With wisdom, biblical accurac

Peter unpacks what it means to

twenty-first century. Whether you are a recent disciple or have
been one for a long time, this book is a must-read, but be warned,
it will challenge and inspire you to die to self and follow Christ
more closely.

Andrew Chard, European Director for AIM International, and formerly,
with his wife Rachel, a pioneer church planter in Africa

The best way to grow as a disciple of Jesus is to share your life
with an experienced and godly Christian. In *Discipleship Matters*
Peter Maiden offers the next best thing, as he invites you to
join him as he describes his walk with God. The result is both
engagingly personal and resolutely biblical. It's a delight to read.
But beware, it's also an exciting challenge.

Tim Chester, Director of Porterbrook Seminary and a pastor with
The Crowded House

As followers of Jesus, we want our worldview to be shaped and
moulded by the Bible. This book is an enormous help in that
process. Starting with the transformation that takes place within
us when we become Christians, and moving through various
aspects of our day-to-day lives, Peter Maiden examines what a
living, dynamic relationship with God looks like. He writes with
integrity, as his life reflects what he believes. Putting his biblical
wisdom into practice will be far from easy, but it will transform
our lives and bring glory to God – because it is all about being a
disciple of the King of kings.

Elaine Duncan, Chief Executive, Scottish Bible Society

Readable, practical, comprehensive in its scope and global in its
vision, this book gives us a challenging and winsome call to
authentic discipleship. It is rich in both biblical reflection and
practical application, but perhaps its most important feature is
that it is written by a man who lives what he teaches.

John Risbridger, Minister and Team Leader of Above Bar Church,
Southampton; Chair of Keswick Ministries

Cutting edge, relevant and a must-read, by someone I have watched and known well over the last forty-five years, and who walks his talk. What a valuable experience to sit at his feet and learn from this great book based on the BOOK of books.

George Verwer, founder of Operation Mobilisation

DISCIPLESHIP
MATTERS

PETER MAIDEN

DISCIPLESHIP MATTERS

Dying to live for Christ

INTER-VARSITY PRESS
Norton Street, Nottingham NG7 3HR, England
Email: ivp@ivpbooks.com
Website: www.ivpbooks.com

© Peter Maiden, 2015

Peter Maiden has asserted his right under the Copyright, Designs and Patents
Act 1988 to be identified as Author of this work.

All rights reserved. No part of this publication may be reproduced, stored
in a retrieval system, or transmitted, in any form or by any means, electronic,
mechanical, photocopying, recording or otherwise, without the prior
permission of the publisher or the Copyright Licensing Agency.

This volume is a completely revised and updated version of the original
Authentic title *Discipleship* published in 2007.

Unless otherwise stated, Scripture quotations are taken from the Holy Bible,
New International Version® Anglicized, NIV® Copyright © 1979, 1984, 2011
by Biblica, Inc.® Used by permission. All rights reserved worldwide.

Scripture quotations marked MSG are from *The Message*. Copyright © 1993, 1994,
1995, 1996, 2000, 2001, 2002. Used by permission of NavPress Publishing Group.

Every effort has been made to trace the source of quoted material in this book.
The publisher apologizes that there are a few omissions, and would be grateful
for notification of any corrections that should be incorporated in future reprints.

British Library Cataloguing in Publication Data
A catalogue record for this book is available from the British Library.

ISBN: 978–1–78359–355–2

Set in Dante 12/15pt
Typeset in Great Britain by CRB Associates, Potterhanworth, Lincolnshire
Printed in Great Britain by Ashford Colour Press Ltd, Gosport, Hampshire

*Inter-Varsity Press publishes Christian books that are true to the Bible and that
communicate the gospel, develop discipleship and strengthen the church for its mission
in the world.*

*Inter-Varsity Press is closely linked with the Universities and Colleges Christian
Fellowship, a student movement connecting Christian Unions in universities and colleges
throughout Great Britain, and a member movement of the International Fellowship of
Evangelical Students. Website: www.uccf.org.uk*

Dedicated to George Verwer,
true disciple and friend

Contents

Keswick Foundations: Series preface

Our prayer was for deep, clear, powerful teaching, which would take hold of the souls of the people, and overwhelm them, and lead them to a full, definite and all-conquering faith in Jesus.

This simple but profound prayer, expressed by Thomas Harford-Battersby as he reported on the 1880 Keswick Convention, explains why hundreds of thousands of Christians the world over have been committed to the Keswick movement. The *purpose* is nothing other than to see believers more wholeheartedly committed to Jesus Christ in every area of life, and the *means* the faithful, clear and relevant exposition of God's Word.

All around the world, the Keswick movement has this purpose and this means. Whether it is to proclaim the gospel, to encourage discipleship, to call for holiness, to urge for mission, to long for the Spirit's empowering or to appeal for unity – hearing God's Word in Scripture is central to fulfilling these priorities. (More information about Keswick Ministries is found at the end of this book.)

Keswick Foundations is a series of books that introduce the priority themes that have shaped the Keswick movement, themes which we believe continue to be essential for the church today. By God's grace, for 140 years the movement has had an impact across the globe, not only through Conventions large and small, but also through a range of media. Books in the Keswick Foundations series provide biblical, accessible and practical introductions to basic evangelical essentials that are vital for every Christian and every local church.

Our prayer for these books is the same as that expressed by Harford-Battersby – that by his Spirit, God's Word will take hold of our souls, leading us to an all-conquering faith in Jesus Christ, which will send us out to live and work for his glory.

Jonathan Lamb
CEO and minister-at-large
Keswick Ministries

Introduction: Cheap grace

He came into my office. I could see that he was disturbed about something. He was in his late twenties, a very successful professional, financially no worries, good at what he did, and still single. The conversation went like this: 'I've come to see you today because I've been asked to take on a leadership role in my local church. Right now, I have no responsibilities in my life that I cannot walk away from. If I accept this invitation, I'm going to lose my independence and my freedom.'

I struggled to know what he was looking for from me. Did he want to hear that it was OK to live the Christian life avoiding responsibility? I think what he wanted to hear was that it was possible to live the Christian life and do exactly what he wanted, when he wanted.

Christianity on the side

What is happening in the Christian church? Some argue that the last twenty-five years have seen the fastest growth in the church since the Holy Spirit was poured out on the day of Pentecost. Church growth statistics from South Korea, China and parts of Africa and Latin America are quite staggering. So why are we not all hugely encouraged? Why are we not seeing the ever-increasing impact of the church in those cultures where this rapid growth is being witnessed?

Almost every Christian leader I speak with, wherever they might be in the world, agrees that the major problem of the day is discipleship. For many, it seems, Christianity is considered to be an 'add-on'. People are living their lives – they hear about Jesus and the salvation he offers, and it sounds good. Preachers promise peace and purpose in life, and even some certainty to help when those nagging fears of death assault us. Some preachers go a lot further and offer all sorts of enticements for 'coming to Jesus': prosperity, health and much more, especially if a contribution to their organization follows. So people add Jesus to the life they already enjoy. And it seems that very little life change is called for other than how we spend an hour on a Sunday morning. In his book *The Scandal of the Evangelical Conscience*,[1] using research produced mainly by George Barna, Ronald Sider exposes the spiritual schizophrenia so evident in much of twenty-first-century American Christianity. It appears that we can happily sing our songs of worship, listen to lots of sermons, but then go out of church to live a life which does not seem substantially different from those where there is no Christian profession at all. Sider shows, for example, that how Christians treat a neighbour of a different ethnicity, or how they treat the sacred covenant of marriage, differs little from the behaviour of those who would not darken the door of a church.

And it's not just an American problem. Christian leaders in every continent that I have visited concur that the challenge we face is helping those who have come to faith to understand that whole-life discipleship is the only reasonable response to the commitment they have made.

Dietrich Bonhoeffer, a young pastor and theologian, wrote his brilliant book *The Cost of Discipleship* in 1937.[2] He believed that German Christians were making terrible and frightening compromises with the evil ideology of Nazism. He argued that the wonderful message of the grace of God, which Martin Luther had rescued, was now being turned into a message which he referred to as 'cheap grace'. He defined this as grace without discipleship. He warned that Christianity had achieved success in Germany, but only by being emptied of its ethical and moral demands.

Is the offer of 'cheap grace' once again in the twenty-first century a danger for the church?

I won't keep you in suspense. The young man who came to my office went on to make good decisions. There were many battles along the way, but he went off to college, obtained a theological degree, and has been involved in church ministry ever since. His life has been transformed by the Holy Spirit as he has obeyed the voice of God. From a drifting, basically selfish, existence, he has given himself to God and ministry to his people. As we shall see, he did not need to go into church ministry to do that, but with his particular gifts, that was the obvious direction for him. We have kept in touch, and it has been fantastic to see him flourishing.

An important principle of discipleship is that the more we give, the more we gain.

Questions

1. 'Jesus is my Saviour, but he is not my Lord.' What do you think of this statement? Is such a thing ever possible?

2. As Bonhoeffer was writing of 'cheap grace', he was witnessing many of his colleagues compromising with the evil of Nazism. What are the danger areas of compromise for you, and for the Christian church today?

Books

Dietrich Bonhoeffer, *The Cost of Discipleship* (SCM, 2001).
Ronald J. Sider, *The Scandal of the Evangelical Conscience: Why Are Christians Living Just Like the Rest of the World?* (Baker, 2005).

Transformed

1

Born again

I recently moved home. Soon afterwards I went along to the nearest gym to sign up for a twelve-month membership. It was possible to join at different levels. Would I be using it every day? Twice a week? Would I attend at weekends? Did I want access any time it was open or wish to avoid peak hours? There was a pool, as well as a gym. Did I want access to both? Different levels of entry for different prices.

Is Christianity like that? Are there different levels of commitment? Different benefits, depending on the price you're willing to pay? Am I even suggesting by what I've said already that, though many become Christians, only some go on to become disciples?

Heart change

Famously, Jesus used the words 'born again' to describe the radical revolution that conversion to Christ entails. He was speaking to a man called Nicodemus, a religious leader with impressive credentials. Nicodemus was a member of the

Sanhedrin, the highest tribunal of the Jews, chaired by the High Priest. He was a Pharisee, and although today Pharisees get bad press, this would have meant that he was a highly respected member of his community. Jesus called him 'Israel's teacher' (John 3:10), which has led some to suggest that he was the most prominent religious leader in his area. Jesus is very clear: 'You must be born again' (John 3:7). You need something more if you're going to be right with God. The words can also be translated: 'born from above'. Jesus is referring to a supernatural experience which is the work of God in the human heart. He's not talking about the alteration of a life, but the revolution, indeed the regeneration, of that life.

Stay with me for a little bit of useful theology! When Adam rebelled against God in the Garden of Eden, he paid the penalty. God had said to him, 'You must not eat from the tree of the knowledge of good and evil, for when you eat from it you will surely die'(Genesis 2:17). But he didn't die. He lived for many years after that fateful act. So what is death? It is separation. When we die physically, a separation takes place:

> The dust returns to the ground it came from,
>   and the spirit returns to God who gave it.
> (Ecclesiastes 12:7)

Adam sinned in the Garden of Eden, and death (of another sort) took place immediately. Adam was separated from God; his life in communion with God had ended.

When we're born again, just as God breathed life into Adam's body and he became a living soul, so he breathes new life into us and we are born again. Communion with God is fully restored. The promise of the new covenant was not that God would give us a new law to keep, but a new heart

(Ezekiel 36:26–27). Yet we cannot have new life without death. We cannot go on living the way we did, with just a few pleasant additions. The old life, our priorities, ambitions and desires all end, and a new life begins. God does this for us in a moment, but it takes a lifetime to appreciate and respond to all that he does in that moment and continues to do throughout our lives.

Communion with God is fully restored.

In days when the term 'born again' is in common use in the media, we must never forget the radical death-and-life nature of this experience: 'Therefore, if anyone is in Christ, the new creation has come: the old has gone, the new is here!' (2 Corinthians 5:17).

Respectable or radical?

One day Jesus met someone who impressed him (Mark 10). He is often referred to as the 'rich young ruler'. When Jesus quoted six of the Ten Commandments to him, he replied, 'All these I have kept since I was a boy' (10:20). Clearly, he had done well in life and made some serious money (verse 22). But he knew that this life, in which he had done so well, was not all there was. He was concerned about life after death and wanted to be sure that all would be well in the future. Had he recognized that Jesus was his answer to this search for assurance about eternity? Was he considering following Jesus as his disciple? Jesus does not offer him an easy road: 'One thing you lack . . . Go, sell everything you have and give to the poor, and you will have treasure in heaven. Then come, follow me' (verse 21). Possessions were clearly going to be the issue for this enthusiastic young man.

Something else might be the issue for me or you, although we have to say that money is often the big issue in our materialistic society. Jesus is not going to be the number two in this man's life. More than that, he's not even going to share first place.

In his book quoted earlier, Ronald Sider writes,

When Christians today reduce the gospel to forgiveness of sins, they are offering a one-sided, heretical message that is flatly unfaithful to the Jesus they worship as Lord and God. Only if we recover Jesus's gospel of the kingdom and allow its power so to transform our sinful selves that our Christian congregations (always imperfect to be sure) become visible holy signs of the dawning kingdom, will we be faithful to Jesus. Only then will our evangelistic words recover integrity and power.[1]

When I was a child, preachers used to talk about people 'being saved'. Then the language changed to 'being converted'. Then it changed again to 'making a decision'. More recently, I hear people being asked to 'make a commitment'. Saved – that is something done for you, an act of God on your behalf. It sounds both urgent and radical. Converted – that is something you can do for yourself, but it still sounds radical. But to make a decision, or a commitment, sounds much more like something you do, and it could be one decision or commitment amongst many.

I'm not advocating the use of outdated language here, but I am very concerned that we appreciate and clearly proclaim that salvation is an act of God. All over the world I have come across people who are trying to be Christians. They have great respect for Jesus. They have read the Sermon on the Mount and even conclude, 'That is how I want to live.' But as we have seen, being a Christian is not about changing your life; it is receiving new life and living in the power of that new life. The danger is that people are trying to be disciples, but have never even been born again.

Word and Spirit

So how does the new birth happen? As we have seen already, it is something God does. We cannot engineer it ourselves. All we can do is respond to what God is doing within us. It is a mysterious work: 'The wind blows wherever it pleases. You hear its sound, but you cannot tell where it comes from or where it is going. So it is with everyone born of the Spirit' (John 3:8). We are 'born of the Spirit', receiving new spiritual life from God as we place our faith in Jesus Christ and turn forever from our sin. We become God's children: 'To all who did receive him, to those who believed in his name, he gave the right to become children of God – children born not of natural descent, nor of human decision or a husband's will, but born of God' (John 1:12–13).

Peter writes, 'For you have been born again, not of perishable seed, but of imperishable, through the living and enduring word of God' (1 Peter 1:23). God's transforming, life-giving power is applied through his Word. We are born again through the Holy Spirit and the Word. James echoes this: 'He chose to give us birth through the word of truth' (James 1:18). Just as the Word of God in creation was life giving, so it is too in the new creation. As we hear or read the Word of truth, and as we are enabled to understand and respond to it by the work of the Holy Spirit, so we are born again. This shows the vital place of Scripture in becoming a disciple, and as we will see in the rest of this book, it is equally vital in our growing as disciples.

The wonderful thing about the Word of the Lord is that it 'endures for ever' (1 Peter 1:25). The seed of God's Word is imperishable. The life within us is eternal life. Does this not make you want to be a diligent student of God's Word? Does it not make you determined to be someone who obeys the Word of God, however counter-cultural it may seem to be? Should we not ensure that in all our witness and preaching, the Word of God has a primary place? At the root of the transformation which takes place in the life of the Christian disciple are the Spirit of God and the Word of God.

New life

When that miracle of new birth takes place, and the new life received is developed, the transformation is total.

Willie 'Pete' Williams from Georgia served more than two decades in prison. He was convicted in 1985 of truly horrific crimes that he had never committed – kidnapping, sodomy and rape – and was sentenced to forty-five years' imprisonment. Williams always claimed his innocence, and the Innocence Project took up the case. After an investigation, they took the case back to court, and in 2007 Williams was found not guilty. After singing a few lines of 'Amazing Grace', forty-four-year-old Williams walked out of prison a free man and went home to eat steak with his family. A few days later he appeared at a news conference and claimed he wasn't angry about spending half his life behind bars. Instead, he demonstrated mercy and forgiveness. 'Anyone can screw up,' he said. 'We're all human.' Williams attributed his remarkable ability to forgive to his conversion to Christ in prison. 'That's been my rock,' he said. His faith in Christ carried him through years of being labelled a sex offender and gave him hope that one day his innocence would come to light.

It's a remarkable story, but Williams was walking in the shoes of his Master: 'Father, forgive them, for they do not know what they are doing' was the prayer of Jesus for those who were crucifying him (Luke 23:34). Williams was behaving as a disciple of Jesus.

On 21 March 2014 it was Mother's Day in Egypt. A programme was shown on Egyptian TV featuring Howida Azer, mother of Miriam, a twelve-year-old girl killed by gunfire from Muslim radicals in front of a church on 21 October 2013. Howida was interviewed, following her daughter's death. She expressed forgiveness to the killers and said she was praying that the Lord would bring them to repentance before they died, and that their eyes would be opened to the truth about the Lord Jesus. The TV presenter was stunned! He said, 'You're an amazing example to the Egyptian people in expressing forgiveness to those who know nothing about forgiveness. Most people whose kids are killed say they won't feel better until they take revenge – until they kill them with their own hands. But you have uttered forgiveness! There is no better example of an Egyptian mother who has this amazing sense of forgiveness for those who killed her daughter. Their hearts have been darkened, yet this mother has completely forgiven them. Even though Miriam's mother came in a wheelchair because of the bullet that hit her body, yet she comes with all this forgiveness and a desire to pray for her attackers.'

'Now,' Miriam's mother concluded, 'if they use a machine gun to kill my daughter, I want to tell the Egyptian people that we believers in the Lord Jesus have an even stronger weapon and that is to fast and pray that God would bring these terrorists to repentance.'[2]

Community changed

Not only are individuals being transformed by the power of
Christ, but communities also. I think of Moqattam garbage
village in Cairo. Go back to 1985, and it was a place where
people lived with their animals and their garbage. No elec-
tricity or running water, no churches, no schools, in fact no
services except for drugs and alcohol – and there was a very
efficient service in both of those commodities. Indeed, the
people considered themselves garbage, and evil and violence
reigned.

Today it's totally different, with high-rise buildings, schools,
churches and markets to greet the eye. What brought about
this total transformation in one generation? The Holy Spirit
used one simple layman who took one simple message into
the village: 'God loves you.' This man first led his garbage
picker to the Lord, and then went with him into the garbage village and shared Jesus with the man's family and
friends. He had no money, no social programme, just
the power of the Holy Spirit. The people responded. As the
number of believers grew, the Coptic Orthodox leaders built
them a small church. Not surprisingly, its members wanted
their layman who had brought them the gospel to be their
pastor. He was ordained Abuna Samaan – 'Father Simon' to
everyone in the village. As the church grew, people were
completely changed from the inside out, by the Holy Spirit.
He gave them a different motivation, and new desires to use
their money to build homes instead of buying alcohol. They
asked for a school, so that their children could learn to read,
even though they themselves couldn't. They became great
recyclers and today are some of the best in the world.

The Holy Spirit continued to lead in amazing ways.
They discovered caves in their village, just a little way up

the mountain. Today these form the world-famous cave churches of Egypt. The larger cave seats up to 20,000 people, making it the largest church anywhere in the Middle East. One of Father Simon's favourite verses is: 'God chose the weak things of the world to shame the strong' (1 Corinthians 1:27). A large fully equipped centre for the disabled and chronically ill is being built, meaning that another of the marginal groups of Egyptian society will be reached with the love of Christ. Moqattam garbage village has become a centre of hope, transformed through the power of the risen Jesus.[3]

Transformation of the total person is at the heart of the gospel message. If responding to the good news of Jesus Christ does not lead us to becoming followers of Jesus, taking him as our model and example, and by the power of the Holy Spirit within us, growing more Christ-like in the way we live, we haven't truly understood it or experienced its power in our lives.

I will now explain how that works out in daily life. I write as a fellow learner and struggler, someone who is in the process of being transformed, hanging on to the promises of Scripture. In the words of 2 Corinthians 3:18, 'We . . . are being transformed into his image with ever-increasing glory, which comes from the Lord, who is the Spirit.'

Questions

1. 'All you need to be converted is to believe in Jesus Christ and invite him into your life.' Is that statement correct? Read James 2:14–26 as you reflect on this question.
2. What does Jesus expect of those who follow him? Read Luke 14:25–33 as you answer.

Books

Graham Hooper, *Undivided: Closing the Faith-Life Gap* (IVP, 2013).

Vaughan Roberts, *Distinctives: Dare to Be Different* (Authentic, 2000).

John Stott, *The Radical Disciple: Wholehearted Christian Living* (IVP, 2013).

It's all about relationship

It's not only Christians who talk about disciples. We hear of the disciples of Eastern mystics, business gurus or even fashion designers. In these cases, being a disciple means following the ideas, the teachings, of your guru. The *Oxford Dictionary* definition of discipleship offers this idea: 'One who takes another as his teacher and model'.

Over the years a large number of discipleship challenges have been placed before me, often considered 'must-do' exercises for those who desire to be true disciples. I've been told I must have a daily quiet time (a time of hearing from God's Word and praying to him), read the Bible through every year (some say twice a year!), spend a minimum of an hour in daily prayer. No day should pass without my sharing my faith with at least one individual. The list goes on. Some of the exercises I found very helpful, others not so helpful. In fact, some drew me towards a legalistic rather than a relational experience with Christ.

Called to relationship

When Jesus spoke of discipleship, he meant all of that, but not in a legalistic spirit, and so much more besides. When we look at the first disciples of Jesus, we see that the call to discipleship was a call to be with him:

> As Jesus was walking beside the Sea of Galilee, he saw two brothers, Simon called Peter and his brother Andrew. They were casting a net into the lake, for they were fishermen. 'Come, follow me,' Jesus said, 'and I will send you out to fish for people.' At once they left their nets and followed him.
> (Matthew 4:18–20)

> As he walked along, he saw Levi son of Alphaeus sitting at the tax collector's booth. 'Follow me,' Jesus told him, and Levi got up and followed him.
> (Mark 2:14)

Jesus' call to discipleship is not an invitation to participate in a programme, or even share in a cause, but to be with a person who can make us into the people he wants us to be. The call is to a relationship that will gradually make us all that God intended us to be. This will be a lifelong process. If we ever think we have got to the end of our discipleship journey and there is no more to learn, then we are in trouble! I have been married to Win for more than forty years and I am still learning new things about myself, and about Win, through this relationship. Don't you think that will be multiplied many times when you are walking with Jesus?

I am so grateful that Jesus has come from the Father and given his life to renew the relationship broken by sin. Discipleship is the outworking of that restored relationship.

By contrast, disciples of business or fashion gurus can follow their ideas without any relationship with them. It can never be that way for the disciple of Jesus. Personal relationship is at the very heart of discipleship. I cannot stress that enough: Christian discipleship can never be just following a teaching or keeping a set of rules or participating in a programme – it is walking through life with a friend.

Christian discipleship . . . is walking through life with a friend.

Called to imitate

In many ways, this relationship is similar to others. It contains the normal stuff of relationships: encouragements and discouragements, progress and setbacks, rewards and disappointments, and discipline too. The disciples in the era of Jesus spent much time with their Master, actually moving and living with him. When they weren't doing that, they were certainly spending hours every day watching him, listening to him and discussing things. Gradually, they took on board the mindset of their Teacher. They began to think as he thought, viewing life the way their Teacher did. And they found themselves gradually reacting to the circumstances of life as their Teacher did. So their worldview gradually became that of their Teacher.

I have seen that in my own life. Admittedly, mine has been flawed and sadly inconsistent, but as I look back, I see that the ways I used to think have been changed through being with Jesus. Some things that I used to value greatly I now consider of far less importance, and some things that I placed little value on are now important to me. I often find myself crying out, 'Lord, why is it taking so long?' But there *has* been change; my worldview has been transformed.

Called to sacrifice

The relationship we enter into with Jesus is the most exciting one we can ever embark on. Imagine those first disciples. They responded to the call to follow Jesus. They left their businesses, their families, to do so. They were with him at a wedding. He's turning water into the best of wines! Now they are in the temple. What is he doing? He's making a whip! He's driving out the money changers and sales staff! Those disciples never knew what a day would bring forth, from the moment they chose to follow Jesus. One reason why this journey is so exciting is because of the scale of its demands. If you're looking for something that demands everything of you, something so special that you would be prepared to die for it, then you're on the right track.

The love-struck couple begin their relationship thinking, 'This is just going to be bliss every day.' But no relationship is ever like that. Jesus was very honest about the price to be paid in being with him. In Luke 14 he used two vivid illustrations to encourage potential followers to evaluate before they committed. If a man is going to build a tower, he doesn't just take bricks and start building. He must sit down and consider things. For example, he may have enough money for the first consignment of bricks, but has he got enough to finish the tower? He's open to ridicule if he runs out of money with half the tower unfinished. What of a king, about to go to war against another king? He discovers that the enemy has twice the number of troops. Does he rush into battle? No, he must seriously consider the situation. Would sending a peace delegation not be the best move? A persuasive preacher may call for an immediate response at the end of an emotionally charged meeting. But such a life-transforming decision cannot be arrived at in a moment. Sit down, said Jesus, there's a price to be paid. Count the cost.

Here are two very similar illustrations where Jesus is clearly concerned to avoid thoughtless decisions that could have serious consequences. However, there is a difference. In the first parable Jesus says sit down and reckon whether or not you can afford to follow me. In the second he says sit down and reckon whether you can afford to refuse my demands.[1] Both of these questions must be faced by anyone considering Christ's call to journey with him.

Called by the King

At the very heart of understanding the call to discipleship is a recognition of the majesty of the person making the call. No-one but the Son of God has the right to make such demands of us, but the Son of God has every right. He has this right because of who he is and what he has done. He is the one to whom every knee will ultimately bow, and through his death he has bought us with a price.

The response of those early disciples was utterly astonishing. Notice that Jesus didn't perform miracles to impress them before issuing his call. He didn't even explain himself or his teaching, or give any idea of what would be involved in following him. Just a simple command: 'Follow me . . . and I will send you out to fish for people' (Matthew 4:19), and immediately they responded, leaving everything behind and going with him. There was something about Jesus which called for that response. Those being addressed immediately knew they could not refuse his demands.

The more we appreciate who Jesus is and all he has done for us, the more we will understand the holy privilege of being called into relationship with him.

Questions

1. To be a disciple is to be with Jesus. What does being with Jesus mean to you?
2. What practical steps could you take to deepen and develop your relationship with God?

Books

J. I. Packer, *Knowing God* (Hodder & Stoughton, 2005).

A. W. Tozer, *The Knowledge of the Holy* (Authentic Classics, 2005).

John Valentine, *Follow Me: Becoming a Liberated Disciple* (IVP, 2009).

3

Dead men walking

Dietrich Bonhoeffer wrote, 'When Christ calls a man, he bids him come and die.'[1] Jesus himself said, 'Whoever wants to save their life will lose it, but whoever loses their life for me will save it' (Luke 9:24).

For Bonheoffer, the call to come and die would lead to a martyr's death. Just before the end of the Second World War, on 8 April 1945, this young theologian and pastor was executed at Flossenbürg Prison. Imagine how he must have felt as he faced martyrdom. He was a brilliant young man. No doubt he was full of hopes, dreams, ambitions and plans as the darkness of Hitler's rule seemed to be coming to its end. Now he realizes that there is no way these dreams can ever be fulfilled. Curtains.

For every disciple of Jesus, death must take place. There is no true life without it. If we think that there is, then we haven't understood what it means to be born again. 'Whoever does not carry their cross and follow me cannot be my disciple' (Luke 14:27). Imagine the scene 2,000 years ago. People are going about their normal duties in town, but suddenly things seem to go quiet. All eyes are turning towards some men struggling up the street carrying large wooden beams on their backs. Everyone knows where they're going: to the place of execution – crucifixion. Everyone knows they're on a one-way journey. No coming back. These men are as good as dead. It's crucial to realize that to follow Christ, I must give up all my plans, ambitions, goals and desires. It's the end of the old life. A new life where I am no longer in charge has begun.

There were those who were interested in following Jesus, but only on their terms. You read about them in Luke 9:57–62: two men whom Jesus met said they wanted to follow him, and another Jesus challenged to follow him. They were clearly not ready to give this relationship the priority it demanded. Yes, they wanted to follow him, but only if the conditions were right. They first wanted to do something else and then they would follow, on their own terms and if it suited their circumstances. But the call to follow Jesus is unconditional. Whatever he asks of me, I cannot refuse. As C. T. Studd said, 'If Jesus Christ be God and died for me, no sacrifice that I make can be too great for me to make for him.'[2]

I was baptized by immersion when I was fourteen years old. Sadly, I did this because it was the expected thing. My peers were being baptized. I didn't want to let family and friends down. The huge significance of this dramatic symbol didn't hit me fully at the time. These days I can never witness a baptism without getting emotional. It's a powerful public statement. It's the end: the death and burial of that old life, with all its sin and selfishness, its ambitions and desires. Rising from the water testifies to the whole new life in Christ which has begun.

'We died with Christ,' writes Paul in Romans 6:8. 'Our old self was crucified with him' (verse 6). What dies when I die with Christ? The person that I used to be, my old self, has died.

When Christ died, he paid the penalty for sin once and for all. We were fully identified with him in that death. We can be absolutely sure that the sin and guilt of that past life have been completely dealt with.

I find that many Christians know that Jesus has dealt with their sin, but they still struggle with their shame. Satan wants us to carry a back-breaking load of guilt through life, but there is absolutely no need to do so. 'The wages of sin is death' (Romans 6:23), and we died with Christ. In Christ, the wages are fully paid. So let's straighten our backs and stand tall.

Alive to God

It takes a daily act of faith to stand tall. It means making the right choices moment by moment. We must 'count [ourselves] dead to sin but alive to God in Christ Jesus' (Romans 6:11).

I love this rendering:

> That means you must not give sin a vote in the way you conduct your lives. Don't give it the time of day. Don't even run little errands that are connected with that old way of life. Throw yourselves wholeheartedly and full-time – remember you've been raised from the dead! – into God's way of doing things. Sin can't tell you how to live. After all, you're not living under that old tyranny any longer. You're living in the freedom of God.
>
> (Romans 6:12–14 MSG)

Life certainly won't be without problems. It's not heaven on earth, not life as I will one day know it, but it is a totally new life with God, the life we were born for, a friendship with the living God! God's promise was: 'I will give you a new heart and put a new spirit in you; I will remove from you your heart of stone and give you a heart of flesh. And I will put my Spirit in you and move you to follow my decrees and be careful to keep my laws' (Ezekiel 36:26–27). Whatever I may feel, whatever Satan might suggest, this is my new reality. And there's a new challenge:

> Since, then, you have been raised with Christ, set your hearts on things above, where Christ is, seated at the right hand of God. Set your mind on things above, not on earthly things. For you died, and your life is now hidden with Christ in God. (Colossians 3:1–3)

Really dead?

The major problem though is that I have received new life, yet my sinful nature lives on. It's very active! This should not take me by surprise. I was not promised when I died with Christ that my sinful nature would be obliterated altogether. I've certainly been promised that from that moment on it would no longer rule my life. I am no longer a 'slave to sin', because anyone who has died has been freed from sin (Romans 6:6–7).

I live in a fallen creation. And I have never been promised that I will be immune from the consequences of living in this fallen creation. I live in a fallen age. All around me is a world dominated by the values and principles that my 'old self' used to hold dear and love. I am seeking to live the life of the eternal age – a lifestyle dominated by totally different values and principles – right in the middle of this fallen world. This is the demanding, but thrilling, challenge of Christian witness. It's a daily struggle, but any disciple who chooses to join the struggle has all the help of God the Holy Spirit who is moving me to 'follow [God's] decrees and to be careful to keep [his] laws' (Ezekiel 36:27). I battle in his strength as I experience his absolutely sufficient power and grace.

Think of the crucifixion. The body is nailed to the cross, but the person is very much alive. In fact, he's fighting with everything he has for survival. The flesh is just like that: crucified but very much alive. I need to take the hammer, and God puts that hammer in my hand, and nail the flesh to keep it on the cross. When the flesh within me seeks to reassert its rule in my life, I must remember my new reality. The flesh has lost its dominant power over me. It has been broken forever by the death and resurrection of Christ and my dying and rising with him. I am free and empowered by the Holy Spirit within me to say 'no'. I must count myself 'dead to sin but alive to God in Christ Jesus' (Romans 6:11).

The great man of faith and founder of orphanages in the nineteenth century, George Müller, said, 'There was a day when I died, *utterly died* ... died to George Müller, his opinions, preferences, tastes and will; died to the world, its approval or censure; died to the approval or blame even of my brethren and friends – and since then I have studied only to show myself approved unto God.'[3]

Communion: Remember me

John Stott writes, 'The Christian life continues where it begins – at the foot of the cross of Jesus. The cross is not an elementary stage which we later grow out of. We never graduate from the school of Calvary. And the Lord's Supper [or Holy Communion, taking bread and wine representing Jesus' body and blood] continuously brings us back to it.'[4]

If baptism, as mentioned earlier, is a powerful symbol, then so too is the Lord's Supper. As we come to the table, we are reminded of just how much we are loved and valued. We are reminded that Jesus died for our sin, and that the guilt and power of sin over us has been forever dealt with, as our old self has died with Christ.

I am also reminded of my responsibilities, which I can now fulfil by the power of the Holy Spirit within me. As my sinful nature seeks to dominate my life again, I am now able, through the finished work of Christ and his resurrection power, to take control. I must refuse the suggestions of the sinful nature, reckon it dead and walk in step with the Holy Spirit who is leading me.

This is the disciple's battleground: 'The flesh desires what is contrary to the Spirit, and the Spirit what is contrary to the flesh. They are in conflict with each other, so that you are not to do whatever you want' (Galatians 5:17). Yet the disciple of Jesus has been truly liberated: 'For we know that our old self was crucified with him so that the body ruled by sin might be done away with, that we should no longer be slaves to sin – because anyone who has died has been set free from sin' (Romans 6:6–7).

It is my passion, the main motive for me in writing this book, that more of Christ's disciples will live in the freedom from the power and shame of sin which Christ died to give to us.

My own Isaac

Sometimes the basic demands of discipleship are placed before you in a way that you cannot dodge. I well remember a forty-eight-hour period when I was afraid that I might lose my son Tim. I spent most of those hours in the hospital room where he was recovering from an operation. There were complications in the recovery process, and something was going on in his body that the medical team could not understand. It was a period of considerable uncertainty and confusion for Win and me, although much more for Tim himself – a traumatic time indeed.

I will never forget wrestling with God. Could I entrust my son to my Father's will? Could I at this critical moment say, 'Thy will be done on earth as it is in heaven'? Or was that just something I repeated in a prayer? Did I only want his will for my life when it suited how I thought life should go?

I was not able just to hand my son over. I fought; I wept; I complained bitterly. 'Have I not sought to serve you as faithfully as I could, Lord? Have there not been sacrifices that I've made for you?' I was slipping into entitlement thinking. Didn't God owe me something? I don't remember all the details of those hours, but at some point I faced the challenge of Abraham. You recall how this man of remarkable faith faced his ultimate test. All his hopes of becoming the father of the great nation which God had promised rested in his son Isaac. Now he is being commanded to sacrifice him.

My situation was very different, but the challenge for me was whether I had the faith of Abraham to release in me the obedience of Abraham. Was I prepared at this point to say, 'Thy will be done'?

It was a long battle in that hospital room. When I finally got there, within a short time the problem was identified, and the crisis was quickly over.

Was I prepared at this point to say, 'Thy will be done'?

I'm very conscious in writing this that others have got to that point possibly far quicker than I did, but have not been blessed with a similar happy outcome. I can only trust that my resolve would have held if my outcome had been different.

But is it really sacrifice?

All of this might seem hugely sacrificial, and I do not want to understate the self-denial involved in following Christ, but is it really sacrifice? When I fell in love with the lady who is now my wife, I often missed the last bus home from her house. It was a long walk. But as I walked, I wasn't thinking that I was a hero. The walk didn't even seem like hard work. The self-denial involved in developing the relationship never entered my head. Paying a price was a joy, the very opposite of a heavy burden. More than forty years later, it's still a joy. When I'm away from home preaching, and there's any possibility of getting home that night, I take it, even if it means hours of driving. It doesn't feel like effort. True disciples of Jesus are likely to be the most joyful, contented people you will ever meet. Just as joy ensues when I seek to do things for Win today, so serving and sacrifice for Jesus is the most satisfying experience in life. It is true that if we 'want to save our lives, we must lose them' (see Matthew 16:25).

Looking forward to eternity

So, a disciple is constantly looking back to the cross, but also looking forwards. In Operation Mobilisation we have a ministry which involves ships. I like to hang over the deck railings as we set sail. Huge ropes are loosened from their moorings, and the ship moves away. And as it leaves dock, preparations are already being made for the next port of call. The captain knows exactly where he is taking the ship.

Paul uses the word 'departure' to describe his imminent death in 2 Timothy 4:6. When he wrote, this maritime image was in his mind. As he died, he knew he would be leaving one shore, but with his Captain in control, he would arrive safely at the next one. This future certainty should be a major influence in our discipleship. A disciple constantly makes choices and decisions by looking back to the cross and forwards to eternity.

Another important biblical picture is that we are travellers, pilgrims walking through this world, with our eyes on our eternal hope. Hebrews 11 records the exploits of remarkable men and women of faith. Key to their lives of faith was the fact that they admitted 'they were foreigners and strangers on earth' (Hebrews 11:13). This understanding did not stop them from making immense contributions in their communities, but as they worked, 'they were longing for a better country – a heavenly one' (Hebrews 11:16).

> *A disciple constantly makes choices and decisions by looking back to the cross and forwards to eternity.*

As you know, I recently moved home. Life in the months leading up to this was interesting. Decisions regarding what we would buy, what we would do in the house or in the community where we lived, were constantly influenced by the realization that we were on the move. Our location was not permanent.

Jesus told us he was going away to prepare our permanent home (John 14:2–3). Are we living like travellers with a rucksack, heading for home? Do we make the daily decisions of life based on that understanding? Martin Luther is reputed to have said, 'There are only two days in my diary: today and that day.' He sought to make the decisions of today in the light of the day when he would stand before Jesus.

For the past forty years I've been travelling all over the world in my role with Operation Mobilisation. To see the inequalities and injustices in our world, the ravages of HIV and, as I write, the Ebola nightmare, poverty and starvation, while personally living in luxury by comparison, has been a challenge. In the midst of all this, the future certainty of 'a new heaven and a new earth, where righteousness dwells' (2 Peter 3:13) has been a great comfort. I'm looking forward to a day when the weak will no longer be abused by the strong, when cancer will exist no more, when death itself will be dead.

Peter shows that we have work to do to bring this day to pass. We can 'speed its coming' (verse 12). This future prospect has to be a great motivation in our mission. The watchword of the pioneers of the modern missionary movement was: 'Let's bring back the King.' Fundamental to their life choices, leading to the most amazing growth of the mission's movement at enormous personal cost, was the conviction of the King's triumphant return. The gospel needed to be preached to all nations, 'and then the end will come' (Matthew 24:14).

The pioneer missionaries travelling in inland Africa did not expect a long life. They were normally young people in their twenties who knew that their ministry would probably last for a year or two before they succumbed to disease. Consequently, they would pack all their belongings not into a suitcase, but in a coffin, and then set sail to Africa. These coffins standing on end with shelves inserted made great cupboards apparently, until required for other duties!

The decision to step onto the ship with your coffin can be understood only by appreciating the depth of their conviction that death was not the end, and that such decisions were part of God's plan to bring back the King to reign 'where righteousness dwells' (2 Peter 3:13).

Our final accountability

This same future prospect must be a huge stimulus to holiness. Peter writes that if you believe these things, 'What kind of people ought you to be?' (2 Peter 3:11). His answer: 'You ought to live holy and godly lives.'

I need people to whom I'm accountable. When I meet with them, I want them to ask probing questions about how I am doing in crucial areas of my life. While the thought that those questions will be asked should not be my primary motive for living a holy life, it is an added motivation. My final accountability, however, will be to the Lord himself, and Peter is clear this is indeed a healthy motivation for holy living: 'Since you are looking forward to this, make every effort to be found spotless, blameless and at peace with him' (verse 14).

There was a period in my life when my priorities were all wrong. I had a great time at school, although I concentrated on sports rather than education. I never went to university, and for years I struggled with that, particularly when I was in the company of those who were a lot better educated than I was. I found myself constantly trying to prove myself, even pretending that I knew things that I didn't so that I would not be seen as a total idiot! The whole focus of my life was wrong.

I needed two things. I needed to look back to the cross and realize my total acceptance by Christ, not on the basis of performance, but through my position as a son. I needed to look forward to the last day, not living driven by what I imagined were the expectations of others, but by the understanding that it will be to the Lord himself that I must give the ultimate account.

When Bonhoeffer knew that he was going to be executed, he said to a friend, 'This is the end . . . for me the beginning of life.' Dr H. Fischer-Hullstrung attended his execution and is quoted as saying,

> At the place of execution, he again said a short prayer and then climbed the steps to the gallows, brave and composed. His death ensued after a few seconds. In almost fifty years that I've worked as a doctor, I can have hardly ever seen a man die so entirely submissive to the will of God.[5]

In a sermon preached in London where Bonhoeffer pastored a church for a time, he said, 'Life only really begins when it ends here on earth . . . all that is here is only the prologue before the curtain goes up.'[6]

Questions

1. 'The doctrine of death to self will lead to the obliteration of our personalities.' Is this true? Can we die to self and still be ourselves?
2. Think back over the last twenty-four hours. Can you recall making any decisions where you chose to die to self and live for Christ? Do you regret any of those decisions?

Books

Paul Mallard, *Invest Your Suffering: Unexpected Intimacy with a Loving God* (IVP, 2013).
David Platt, *Radical: Taking Back Your Faith from the American Dream* (Random House, 2010).
Tom Wright, *Surprised by Hope* (SPCK, 2007).

4

Who do you think you are?

A few years ago I had many titles. I was the International Director of OM, Chairman of the Keswick Convention, Co-chair of a Bible college and a board member of Biblica (a global Bible translation and distribution ministry).

Today I have none of those titles; I've retired from all these positions. So who am I? It is so critical as Christian disciples that our identity is not found in our position, our work, achievements or in anything other than the fact that we are sons and daughters of God. That's a title that can never be bettered or lost! And this realization brings incredible freedom. You no longer have to do things to prove yourself, to make a name for yourself. You are now fully free to serve God and his people. The need to be self-serving is gone.

Jesus and his disciples are having supper. They have now been with him for three years, listening to him and watching him constantly. Proper etiquette demands that guests with dusty feet from their journey should have them washed before eating. But this is not a pleasant task. Just come with me into any OM men's dormitory and you will understand! The task is reserved for the servant in the house. Imagine the scene: everyone knows what should happen, but as the minutes pass, no-one makes the move. No-one reaches for the water and towel. Who is sufficiently secure to serve? Who is so sure about his own position that he's freed up to take the servant role?

As the tension rises, in a moment you would imagine the disciples remembered for the rest of their lives, Jesus takes that servant position. Peter, it seems, sees the significance of that moment: 'Lord, are you going to wash my feet?' (John 13:6). Is there a sense of embarrassment as he asks the question? The Lord of heaven and earth within a short time will say to these same men, 'All authority in heaven and on earth has been given to me' (Matthew 28:18). He's washing the feet of fishermen and tax collectors. What the disciples were unwilling to do for each other, Jesus is doing for all of them.

The key to this wonderful freedom is found in John 13:3. The foot washer is described as the one who 'had come from God and was returning to God'. Totally secure in his identity, Jesus freely pours out his life in service.

'Follow my example'

He tells his disciples why he did this for them: 'I have set you an example that you should do as I have done for you' (verse 15). Jesus was saying here, 'This is how I want you to live. I want you to be towel grabbers – constantly looking for opportunities to take the towel of service.' If this is not our heart attitude, then we are placing ourselves above our Master, who said, 'Now that I, your Lord and Teacher, have washed your feet, you also should wash one another's feet' (verse 14).

In previous chapters we've thought of some of the biblical principles that undergird discipleship. How do these work out in everyday life? This attitude of towel-grabbing service is, I believe, one of the fundamental ways.

The Lord Jesus is our supreme example of servanthood. This foot washing was a symbolic act: Jesus is cleansing the dirty feet of his disciples with water, but he will go on from supper to provide cleansing with blood for dirty, sinful lives. This is why Jesus says to Peter, 'You do not realise now what I am doing, but later you will understand' (verse 7). This foot washing was symbolic of the greatest act of service this planet would ever witness.

> *This foot washing was symbolic of the greatest act of service this planet would ever witness.*

What's in your mind?

When someone does something that surprises us, we might ask, 'What was in his or her mind?' What was in the mind of Christ as he approached the cross? What drove him forward, even when his heart was in anguish (John 12:27)? Paul explains that there was no thought of position or power in the mind of Jesus:

> . . . who, being in very nature God,
>   did not consider equality with God
>   something to be used to his own advantage;
> rather, he made himself nothing.
> (Philippians 2:6–7)

The servant heart that led Jesus to the cross must be our mindset too.

Service was in the mind of Christ as he approached the cross. The opportunity to serve his Father and humanity in rebellion against him was in his mind. As he moved around the table, he came to Judas Iscariot. Jesus knew full well of his betrayal plans (John 13:11). Will he pass him by? Surely we are not called to serve our betrayers? But no feet are missed! This is our calling as disciples. We follow the one who grabbed the towel to serve even his betrayer.

Do you have a Judas in your life? Is God calling you to wash his or her feet?

Many years ago I endured my most difficult year in Christian ministry. In short, a colleague was out to get me. He was a very sincere brother, but he had completely misunderstood some of my actions. Nothing I could say or do would convince him that I was for him. He was sure I was against him, and at all costs I had to go. I knew my calling. I had to serve him – to wash his feet. But was it possible? Sadly, I cannot say that I succeeded on all occasions, but Jesus does not call us to do the impossible. Without steps of faith, without utilizing the gifts given to us by the Holy Spirit, it is totally impossible, but these gifts have been given to us, so our calling is 100% clear.

Everything must go

One of the biblical pictures of this life of service is that of the disciple as a steward or manager. It was in my late teens that I was first challenged by surely one of the most remarkable statements Jesus ever made: 'Those of you who do not give up everything you have cannot be my disciples' (Luke 14:33). I didn't like the black-and-white nature of that statement, so I looked at all the translations to see if they might introduce a shade of grey! In the end I had to conclude that this was exactly what Jesus had said. To follow him as his disciple, everything had to go. Initially, I thought Jesus was speaking just about possessions, and I'm sure that was in his mind, but a lot more than possessions have to go if we truly are to follow Jesus. As we have seen, death must take place, and that includes death to all the dreams and ambitions of our old lives. Dallas Willard writes,

We cannot but serve our treasures. We labour all day for them and think about them all night. They fill our dreams. But it is not uncommon for people to think that they can treasure this world *and* an invisible kingdom as well, that they can serve both. Perhaps we can make this work for a while. But there will come a time when one must be subordinate to the other. We simply cannot have two ultimate goals or points of reference for our actions. That is how life is, and no one escapes. You cannot be the servant of both God and 'things on earth', because their requirements conflict. Unless you already put God first, for example, what you will have to do to be financially secure, impress other people, or fulfil your desires will inevitably lead you against God's wishes. That is why the first of the Ten Commandments, 'You shall have no other gods who take priority over me,' is the first of the Ten Commandments.[1]

But we all have possessions. And God has given us gifts and abilities. How are we to view these?

First, we must use what we have for God as his stewards. Jesus told a parable about a man with servants. This man went on a journey and he divided his property. We can probably think of it in terms of giving each servant a certain amount of money. One was given five talents, another two and another one. The five-talent man went to look for work and soon he had ten. The two-talent man did equally well and doubled his money. The one-talent man just dug a hole and hid what he had been given, preserving it for his master's return. The profit makers were rewarded, while the hole digger was not.

We are to go to work with what we have as servants and stewards to build up and extend our Master's kingdom. You might feel that you are only a one-talent man or woman, with not much to offer. You're probably doing yourself an injustice here because, as we shall see later, God gives gifts to all his servants. The challenge is to use what we have, not to long for what we do not have. The response the master gives to the man who now has four talents and the man who has ten is exactly the same. They've used what they were given to the full. What we have is ours for a greater purpose. The purpose is not self-indulgence, but extending our Master's rule.

Secondly, we can choose to live simply so that we are able to give generously. For those of us in the Western world, this is a particular challenge. When we think of the inequalities between those in the developed and undeveloped world, surely a percentage of our income should be used to balance that inequality. I often wonder whether one of the most serious failures in the Western church is that of not responding adequately to this imbalance.

Thirdly, community was the pattern in the early church: 'All the believers were one in heart and mind. No one claimed that any of their possessions was their own, but they shared everything they had' (Acts 4:32). God may call some of us to live in community today. But even though that may be the calling for only a few, there should still be caring and sharing amongst Christ's disciples. If we consider the New Testament picture of the church as a body, we remember that when one limb hurts, the whole body is affected. I am a bit of a runner, and as the years pass, injuries increase. I know that when I injure a muscle, the rest of the body compensates for that weakness. I must be careful that there isn't an over-compensation leading to further injury. That is how the members of the body of Christ should respond to those in need, with an enthusiasm to care and share.

Ananias and Sapphira belonged to this community in the early church. They owned a piece of land, but they sold it and gave part of the money from the sale to the apostles, no doubt to share with the community. It seems, however, that they made it appear that they were giving everything from the sale. Now, there was no compulsion for them to give everything. Their sin was not the amount they gave, but their deceit. And they came under the judgment of God because of that deceit. Peter said to Ananias, 'Didn't it belong to you before it was sold? And after it was sold, wasn't the money at your disposal?' (Acts 5:4).

The legitimacy of ownership for a disciple is clearly taught here. But it is always ownership for a purpose. God gives me things to use for his glory: my house, car, bank balance, mind, gifts, abilities, body – all are his. I have been bought at a price (see 1 Corinthians 6:20).

In the second part of this book, we will look at some of the things God gives us and how we should use them for him. Now might be a good time to pause and list your possessions and think of how they might be used for kingdom extension. I have said already that it's not all about material possessions, but the thing about them is that their use is very quantifiable and often a good indicator of where our heart lies.

Questions

1. Do you have the equivalent of a Judas in your life, and is God calling you to wash his or her feet?

2. Look at the diagrams that follow. Fill in where you serve already and ask God if he would like to see the diagrams change.

Where are you serving? Where else is God calling you to serve?

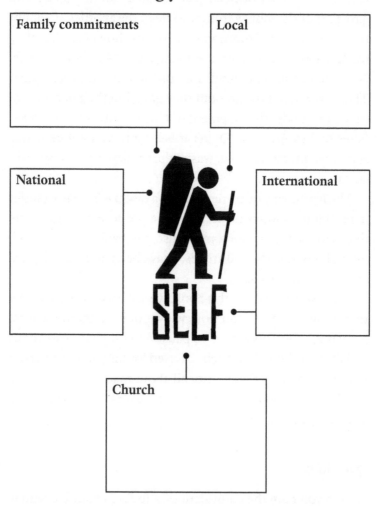

Example: your commitments might look like this:

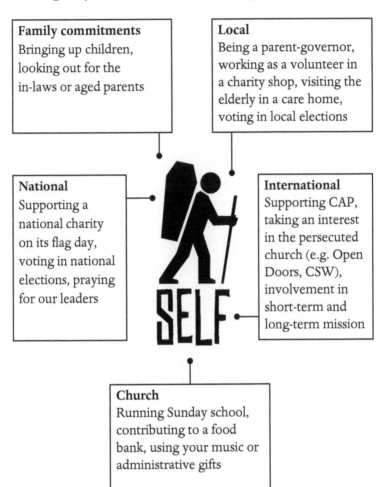

Family commitments
Bringing up children, looking out for the in-laws or aged parents

Local
Being a parent-governor, working as a volunteer in a charity shop, visiting the elderly in a care home, voting in local elections

National
Supporting a national charity on its flag day, voting in national elections, praying for our leaders

International
Supporting CAP, taking an interest in the persecuted church (e.g. Open Doors, CSW), involvement in short-term and long-term mission

Church
Running Sunday school, contributing to a food bank, using your music or administrative gifts

Books

John Stott, *Calling Christian Leaders* (IVP, 2002).
Eric Metaxas, *Bonhoeffer: Pastor, Martyr, Prophet, Spy* (Thomas Nelson, 2011).

5

The Holy Spirit: Fruit and gifts

I grew up in an era when certain parts of the church seemed almost to fear the subject of the Holy Spirit. Controversy raged over whether you received the Holy Spirit when you were born again, or whether a second experience, a baptism of the Holy Spirit, was essential. What was the evidence that you had received the Holy Spirit? Did you need to speak in tongues to be sure? The controversy got really hot, so some felt that it was best to go silent on the subject. Consequently, in some parts of the church, the Holy Spirit was referred to as 'the forgotten member of the Holy Trinity'.

How could we ever become silent about the Holy Spirit and his work in our lives?

How could we ever become silent about the Holy Spirit and his work in our lives? The mind-blowing truth is that God lives in us! Our bodies are the temples in which he has chosen to live. It is God the

Holy Spirit who guides us and empowers us to live the life of discipleship.

In this vital chapter we will look at the work of the Holy Spirit in our lives today, the gifts he gives us and the fruit he bears within us.

In Isaiah 44:3 God says,

> I will pour water on the thirsty land,
>   and streams on the dry ground;
> I will pour out my Spirit on your offspring,
>   and my blessing on your descendants.

But the Holy Spirit was already active in the Old Testament. He was active in creation, revelation (revealing God's truth and his will through his servants; see e.g. Numbers 24:2), regeneration (the gift of new life from God; see e.g. Ezekiel 11:19), equipping the people of God for particular tasks, and much more. So what did Isaiah mean? A day was coming – and many other prophets made the same point – when God would give the gift of his Spirit in a new and distinctive way. He would be available to everyone, all the time. The days in which we are living are called in Scripture: 'the age of the Spirit'. John the Baptist said, 'I baptise you with water, but he will baptise you with the Holy Spirit' (Mark 1:8).

Receive the gift

Jesus does two wonderful things for us. He takes away our sins and baptizes us with the Holy Spirit. Peter concludes his sermon on the day of Pentecost thus: 'Repent and be baptised, every one of you, in the name of Jesus Christ for the forgiveness of your sins. And you will receive the gift of the Holy Spirit' (Acts 2:38).

The Acts of the Apostles shows the difference that the gift of the Spirit made to those disciples. From a fearful bunch of men forsaking Jesus in his hour of need, fleeing for their lives, they became a group of fearless men, loyal to Jesus, even if it meant death – which it eventually did for many of them. The gift of the Holy Spirit, living now within them, made all the difference.

Today's disciples enjoy the same gift. Ever since Pentecost, wherever God's people have gone, his Spirit has gone with them, continuing to do God's work through them. The primary work of the Holy Spirit is to make known to us the presence of the risen Jesus in his people and in the world. Jesus said of him, 'He will glorify me because it is from me that he will receive what he will make known to you' (John 16:14). This means that the Holy Spirit would teach the disciples the truth about Jesus when he was no longer with them. He would be constantly showing them the majesty of the person they were serving and following. But the Holy Spirit does even more than that: 'Jesus went on to say, "In a little while you will see me no more, and then after a little while you will see me"' (verse 16). Jesus was going away, but not for long! The Holy Spirit would bring Christ himself to those who were following him.

That was what made all the difference for those early disciples: from fear to faith because they knew that the Christ they had watched die (from a distance) was now alive and with them. They knew this through the work of the Holy Spirit.

How grateful we should be that we're not called to follow Jesus just by our own human resolve. The Holy Spirit, the Spirit of Jesus, is with us as we walk the road. Our task as we walk is to 'keep in step with the Spirit' (Galatians 5:25).

Although we can never be sure where he might lead us, and he has never promised an easy journey, walking in step with him is a joy because of the way he leads. As Charles Spurgeon said, 'Being led by the Spirit is a remarkable expression. The Bible doesn't say, "As many as are driven by the Spirit of God". No, the devil is a driver.' The Holy Spirit leads and encourages us.

Go on being filled!

But why then, with the Holy Spirit within us, does the Christian life sometimes seem to be such hard graft? Why do I so often fail to experience the power clearly available to me?

There are many reasons, not least that often we do not enjoy the presence and power of the Spirit in the way God intends us to do. In Ephesians 5:18 Paul writes, 'Be filled with the Spirit.' The tense of the verb means that we are *to go on being* filled with the Spirit. This is not something that happens once at conversion, and no more attention is required. It is a lifelong process. The actual meaning of the statement is: 'Let the Holy Spirit fill you.' There is no course you have to go through to learn a technique to receive the Spirit. The Holy Spirit will go on filling you as you, by faith, ask him to do so and avoid grieving him.

Are you making this request regularly: 'Please go on filling me today, Lord, with your Holy Spirit, and help me to avoid anything in my life which will grieve him'? It is interesting that in the parallel passage in Colossians, Paul writes, 'Let the message of Christ dwell among you richly' (Colossians 3:16). The way to be sure you do not grieve the Holy Spirit is to live in obedience to the message of Christ, the Word of God. As he is the Holy Spirit, living a holy life will bring him joy, rather than grief.

Fruit and gifts

As we ask God to go on filling us with his Spirit, fruit is born in our lives. The Holy Spirit makes the presence of Christ known, and as we walk in step with the Spirit, Christ-like characteristics will become evident.

Paul gives us the beautiful fruit of a Spirit-filled life in Galatians 5:22: 'But the fruit of the Spirit is love, joy, peace, forbearance, kindness, goodness, faithfulness, gentleness and self-control.' Paul is not giving us a moral code or a new law by which we must strive to live. As we 'go on being filled with the Spirit', this fruit will be the natural outcome in our lives. You will see from this list that every part of our lives will be affected. John Stott writes, 'The primary direction of "love, joy, peace" is Godward, of "patience, kindness, goodness" manward, and of "faithfulness, gentleness and self-control", selfward.'[1] Truly a life transformed by the Holy Spirit's power. This fruit bearing is the essence of discipleship as we walk in step with the Spirit.

And this fruit is also the evidence of discipleship. Jesus taught that if you want to distinguish between a genuine disciple and a false prophet, the fruit displayed in their lives is what you must examine:

> Watch out for false prophets. They come to you in sheep's clothing, but inwardly they are ferocious wolves. By their fruit you will recognise them. Do people pick grapes from thorn-bushes, or figs from thistles? Likewise, every good tree bears good fruit, but a bad tree bears bad fruit. A good tree cannot bear bad fruit, and a bad tree cannot bear good fruit.
> (Matthew 7:15–18)

Along with the fruit come gifts of the Spirit. And everyone to whom God gives the gift of his Spirit receives spiritual gifts.

Yes, everyone! I know some Christians who don't believe this. They feel they have very little to offer to the body of Christ. And I know many more who don't believe it enough! Not enough of us go to work to discover, develop and deploy our gifts to the full. Paul tells the Corinthians, 'To each one the manifestation of the Spirit is given for the common good' (1 Corinthians 12:7). When we receive the Holy Spirit, he doesn't lie dormant within us. He will show himself, and in the context of 1 Corinthians it's clear that Paul means he will show himself as we use the gifts that he gives us.

It is very important to understand what a spiritual gift is. Eugene Peterson paraphrases 1 Corinthians 12:7: 'Each person is given something to do that shows who God is' (MSG). Jim Packer says, 'Spiritual gifts are actualized powers to express, celebrate, communicate Christ in one way or another by word or deed.'[2]

Christians may have great abilities, but if they use those abilities in ways which do not draw people to Christ, they are not using a spiritual gift. Remember that the Holy Spirit will always glorify Christ. Displaying the fruits of the Spirit and developing the gifts of the Spirit must go hand in hand. Otherwise there is a danger that these gifts will be used for self-glorification and advancement. Sadly, I am sure all of us can point to situations where that has been the case, and it's invariably a tragedy both for the individual and for the testimony of Christ.

Samson was given exceptional gifts, but he simply didn't have the maturity of character to handle them. He was an accident waiting to happen and he crashed time and time again. Eventually, we have the tragic picture of this highly gifted man with his eyes gouged out by the Philistines, bound in shackles, being used as entertainment and as a reason to praise their gods (Judges 16:23–25).

When Philip the evangelist went to Samaria, there was a great turning to God. A well-known figure in the area, Simon, who practised magic, followed Philip wherever he went. He was astonished by the miracles that he witnessed, but . . . 'When Simon saw that the Spirit was given at the laying on of the apostles' hands, he offered them money and said, "Give me also this ability so that everyone on whom I lay my hands may receive the Holy Spirit"' (Acts 8:18–19). Peter's response was: 'May your money perish with you, because you thought you could buy the gift of God with money!' (verse 20).

It has been said that spiritual gifts are 'tools to be used, not toys to be played with'.

What is your gift?

It got to the point where I had to make a decision. Every lunchtime and coffee break at work I would hide away preparing my next sermon. I was being asked to preach in churches and chapels all around the area. Not only was I being asked once, but I was being invited to return, and organizers were passing on my name to other chapels too.

I joined Operation Mobilisation initially on a short-term team in Spain. I was asked to be the bookkeeper. What a disaster! They took the job from me before long. Detailed figures are just not my thing.

Over many years of serving the church and Operation Mobilisation, what was increasingly obvious in the early days has since been confirmed. Ask me to preach and teach, and I rise to the opportunity. It's where I feel comfortable and fulfilled. But in my leadership in OM, I have always needed colleagues to pick up the details of the bigger issues I have been dealing with. I am just not a detail person. Without those colleagues using their gifts, my leadership would never have flourished.

What comes to your mind when you think of a gifted Christian? Do you think of a powerful preacher or a gifted worship leader? Such people certainly do have spiritual gifts. At one church where I worshipped for more than forty years we had a treasurer who looked after things with minimum fuss and great efficiency. Was he exercising his spiritual gift? Of course. The manner in which he did it didn't promote himself, and the confidence we all had in him allowed the church to get on with the business of bringing glory to Christ.

A good exercise is to look at the Scripture passages that cover spiritual gifts, and make a list. (See the questions at the end of this chapter.) You will probably be surprised at the variety. The study will confirm that preaching is indeed a spiritual gift, but the gift of administration is there also, as well as hospitality and serving. And I don't think that all spiritual gifts are mentioned in the Bible. I have a friend who has a terrific gift of writing songs that teach the truths of the Bible. I think Charles Wesley had that gift as well!

Just as you ask the Lord to fill you with his Holy Spirit, ask him to reveal the spiritual gift he has given to you. Conversation with those who know you well might be an important part of the process of discovery. Getting busy in Christian work is also vital in this process. But don't think you can't do anything until you know what your gifts are. Get busy, and your gifts will soon become evident. Don't think that once you know your gifts, you will never do anything that doesn't require those gifts. Sometimes we just have to do things we're probably not gifted to do because the job needs to be done!

Your gifts will need to be developed. Once you realize what your gifts are, you might check out any training opportunities available in that ministry area. Are there others you know with that gift from whom you could learn? In the early days, when my preaching was developing, a couple of experienced preachers took me under their wing. When they had an invitation to preach, they would take me with them and we would discuss the sermon as we travelled there and back. Don't you think it would be a tremendous service to the church if everyone using their spiritual gifts in ministry would take at least one apprentice under their wing? This would lead to much greater gift development and far smoother transitions.

The Christian disciple is someone in whom the fruit of the Spirit is increasingly evident, using God-given gifts to make Christ's glory known. It's a thrilling prospect. Christ ministering through us, by his Spirit within us, using our lives and our abilities as his. We become his mouth, his hands and his feet in this world.

Questions

1. Are you asking the Lord to go on filling you with the Holy Spirit? Can you identify anything in your life that might be grieving him?
2. Make a list of the spiritual gifts mentioned in Romans 12:6–8; 1 Corinthians 12:7–11; and 1 Peter 4:9–11. Study each gift and seek to define it. Can you see examples of these gifts being used in your church?

Books

Gordon D. Fee, *Paul, the Spirit and the People of God* (Hodder & Stoughton, 1997).

J. I. Packer, *Keep in Step with the Spirit: Finding Fullness in Our Walk with God*, 2nd edn (IVP, 2005).

All of life

6

Mind the gap

I left a job in the commercial world to give the whole of my time to teaching and preaching, and eventually, to the leadership role I mentioned, in Operation Mobilisation. When I made that move, was I going from the secular world into Christian ministry? That's how many Christians would describe it, but this thinking is evidence of a tragic misunderstanding that is the biggest enemy of Christian discipleship apart from Satan himself.

Over the years I have interviewed a large number of candidates considering joining Operation Mobilisation. I ask them, 'Why are you considering this?' Many times the answer has been: 'I feel I spend so much valuable time at work. Now I want to do something really worthwhile with the whole of my time.' The only truly worthwhile way of occupying your time is considered to be as the staff member of a church or a Christian organization.

The fatal divide

Separating life into the sacred and the secular in this way is dividing what God has joined together. The two should never be separated. While our theology would say that 'all of life is important to God', it is clear from our practice that we actually believe that some parts of life matter far more than others. Consequently, some of our activities are holy and sacred: church and quiet time, for example, while other parts of life are at best neutral: work, leisure and sleep, to name three.

This critical misunderstanding risks making us appear to be two people in one. A set of values rules our lives on Sundays at worship or in our quiet times on Monday morning. Quite another set rules our thinking when making business decisions in the office, responding to the boss on the factory floor or preparing to make a tackle on the football field.

One unforgettable day in November 1989, the Berlin Wall, which had divided two peoples living by completely different cultural values, came crashing down. Similarly, this division, where one set of values rules one part of our lives and a different set rules another, must be razed to the ground. If we fail to bring down this wall, the sad consequence is that our witness in the world as Christians will be damaged.

Are we not all guilty, to a greater or lesser degree, of this compartmentalizing of our lives? We use phrases like our 'business lives' or our 'family lives' or our 'church lives'. The stand-out characteristics in the life of Jesus, by contrast, were integrity, authenticity and wholeness. Testifying to Theophilus of Jesus' life, Dr Luke writes, 'about all that Jesus began to do and to teach' (Acts 1:1). There was no division between word and deed; belief and practice went hand in hand.

One consequence of this compartmentalization can be the privatization of our faith: we keep it within certain parts of our lives. It is something we turn on at certain times and turn off at others.

There is so much that we can learn from the growing church in continents like Africa. A pastor there recently commented on the differences between churches in the UK and Africa. He explained that for many African Christians, God is a reality that is part of their everyday lives. They will pray on trains and buses when they are travelling. They not only dedicate their children to the Lord at birth, but they also dedicate their new car or their new home. African spirituality, he explained, is woven into the everyday realities of life. This pastor was concerned that for many Western Christians, God is reduced to two hours in a Sunday service. He commented, 'If we believe that God is involved in the whole of our lives, then he has to be seen in public. In Africa and indeed other places like Asia and the Caribbean, shops will have names such as "Amazing Grace" or "God's blessings" shop and "Almighty God" barbers shop. For Africans, God has to be public; he cannot be reduced to our private lives or private spaces.'

Our relationship with God cannot be confined to our churches or homes. The consequence of compartmentalization and privatization is disempowerment. We lose our confidence in the gospel. Will it really stand up in the public square? I am not, of course, advocating that we start giving 'Christian' names to our businesses; rather, I am showing the serious consequences of compartmentalization and its inevitable results of privatization and disempowerment.

Scholars believe that this sacred-secular divide had its roots in the early Greek scholars like Plato, who introduced the idea of dualism, a notion that life can be divided into physical and spiritual realms. This doctrine of the two lives is expressed by Eusebius of Caesarea (265–339), who

> . . . distinguished a perfect form 'beyond common human living' from a secondary form which allowed for 'farming

for trade and the other secular interests.' Augustine praised
farmers, craftsmen and even merchants, but he still tended
to treat these activities as less than contemplation: 'The
one is loved, the other endured.' For Thomas Aquinas
'the life of contemplation was still better than the life
of action.'[1]

This divide leads to the view that some callings in life are
sacred, and therefore more important than those which
are secular. So the missionary or the minister is admired, and
seen as privileged to have such 'ministry', while the teacher,
the administrator or the housewife is taken up with a lesser
calling. How can it be that the Sunday school teacher who
teaches ten children, mainly from Christian backgrounds, for
thirty minutes once a week, is prayed for in this role within
the church, but there is no mention of his or her 'secular' role
in a school as a teacher, interacting for many hours each week
with 3,000 children, mainly from a non-Christian background?
Those called to 'full-time service' are invited to the front of
the church to be commissioned and prayed for by church
leaders, while those who go daily into schools, offices and
factories as Christ's representatives receive no such recognition and support.

Into the ministry?

The word 'ministry' suffers similarly. In a church that I used
to attend, those responding to the call to full-time service
were invited to come to the front of the church for the elders
to lay hands on them and commission them. Then there was
a significant change. Every member of the church at some
point in the year was invited to the front and commissioned
into ministry: one week it was the health service workers, next

education and the next mothers and fathers. Listen to John Stott on this subject:

> We do a disservice to the church whenever we refer to the pastorate as 'the ministry', for example when we speak of ordination in terms of 'entering the ministry'. This use of the definite article implies that the ordained pastorate is the only ministry there is. But *diakonia* is a generic word for service; it lacks specificity until a descriptive adjective is added, whether 'pastoral', 'social', 'political', 'medical' or another. All Christians without exception, being followers of him who came 'not to be served but to serve', are themselves called to ministry, indeed to give their lives in ministry. But the expression 'full-time Christian ministry' is not to be restricted to church work and missionary service; it can also be exercised in government, the media, the professions, business, industry and the home. We need to recover this vision of the wide diversity of ministries to which God calls his people.[2]

Rethink urgently required

There are many other consequences of this divide. It can, for example, lead us to view sex as a far-from-holy activity! We are considered to be made of two parts: the body which is unholy and bound for destruction, and the soul or spirit which is pure and eternal. To be holy is to be separate from the world, a world where you have no calling to influence. Heaven, of course, is far more important than earth, which has no future. Our hope is that we will be snatched away one day from this earth 'to meet the Lord in the air' (1 Thessalonians 4:17). This present world, many Christians believe, is reserved for destruction, and our only hope is to escape it.

But the Bible is very clear that God made a good world. He placed it under a curse because of human sin, but he promised that creation would one day be renewed and restored. We look forward to eternity in a new heaven and a new earth (2 Peter 3:13). But this is new in nature and in quality, not in origin. Theologian Anthony Hoekema writes, 'What Peter teaches here is not the emergence of a cosmos totally other than the present one, but the creation of a universe which, though it has been gloriously renewed, stands in continuity with the present one.'[3]

The result of this divide is that our faith doesn't relate to and inform the whole of our lives while relegated to importance only in 'spiritual' areas.

Paul tells Timothy that in 'later times', which means his day and ours, 'some will abandon the faith' and follow false teachers:

> They forbid people to marry and order them to abstain
> from certain foods, which God created to be received with
> thanksgiving by those who believe and who know the truth.
> For everything God created is good, and nothing is to be
> rejected if it is received with thanksgiving, because it is
> consecrated by the word of God and prayer.
> (1 Timothy 4:3–5)

Here is a typical example of the sacred-secular divide. Many of these early false teachers who troubled the Christian church can be grouped together under the title of 'Gnostics'. The essence of Gnosticism was that the spirit is altogether good, and matter altogether evil. Many of these groups also believed that the kingdom of God had already come in its fullness. They wanted to enjoy what God had promised them in the future right there and then. What use had they for material things if salvation was fully obtainable now? You could do what you like with your body; it was no longer important!

The issues that we will look at next are all affected by this false, unbiblical and dangerous dichotomy. But it has been so much part of Christian thinking for so long that we will need to ask God to renew our minds and help us to see life as God sees it.

For that renewal to take place, we must appreciate the sovereignty of God over the whole of life. Abraham Kuyper, Prime Minister of the Netherlands from 1901 to 1905, famously said, 'No single piece of our mental world is to be hermetically sealed off from the rest, and there is not a square inch in the whole domain of our human existence over which Christ, who is Sovereign over *all*, does not cry: "Mine!"'[4] This is Paul's theme in Colossians 1:15–20: Christ is Lord over all. He is the cosmic Christ. His opponents in Colossae may have rejected the 'material' for the 'spiritual', but for followers of the King of kings, there can be no such division. His rule is over all things. God's ultimate goal for a fallen creation is the reconciliation of all things (verse 20). The church must be a demonstration of this holistic reconciliation. When we divide what should never be separated, our testimony in a fallen world is destroyed.

This holistic reconciliation was certainly the vision of the Old Testament prophets: we see some beautiful pictures of creation redeemed. Global warming is leading to the rapid expansion of desert, with tragic consequences, but as we battle to reverse this, we know that one day it will be fully reversed:

> The desert and the parched land will be glad;
> the wilderness will rejoice and blossom.
> Like the crocus, it will burst into bloom;
> it will rejoice greatly and shout for joy.
> (Isaiah 35:1–2)

The wolf will live with the lamb,
    the leopard will lie down with the goat,
the calf and the lion and the yearling together . . .
    and the lion will eat straw like the ox.
The infant will play near the cobra's den,
    and the young child will put its hand into the viper's nest.
They will neither harm nor destroy
    on all my holy mountain,
for the earth will be filled with the knowledge of the LORD
    as the waters cover the sea.
(Isaiah 11:6–9)

God is sovereign over all of his creation. He is committed to redeeming his fallen creation.

So God is involved in the whole of our lives. In the pattern prayer given to his disciples, Jesus teaches us to pray for his Father's name to be hallowed, his kingdom to come, and his will to be done on earth as it is in heaven. But immediately, he moves on to teach that we should be asking our Father for our daily bread. Some have asked, 'How can Jesus move so quickly from such huge weighty issues to such seemingly mundane matters?' Simple answer: all of our lives are important to God; he is involved in every part. He does not compartmentalize in the way that we are prone to do. This is wonderfully liberating truth! Everything we do is important to God, and he is involved with us in it all.

The renewal which we so desperately need in the Western church must start with the individual. Is there an integrity, a wholeness about my Christian life? Am I one thing in the home and church, but quite another at my place of work or leisure? I was travelling on a train, and a lurid conversation was going on right behind me as two men discussed the price of prostitutes in different European cities. I got up to go to the buffet and immediately recognized one of the men as an elder of a church where I had been preaching the previous Sunday.

This example may seem extreme, but Jesus spoke about this double life which we can so easily slip into. He said of the Pharisees that they honoured him with their lips, but their hearts were far from him (Matthew 15:8).

Questions

1. Do you see any evidence of this secular-spiritual divide in your life? Where?
2. Why are so many Christians so private about their faith?

Books

Mark Greene, *Thank God It's Monday: Ministry in the Workplace* (Scripture Union, 1994).

Julian Hardyman, *Maximum Life: All for the Glory of God* (IVP, 2009).

Graham Hooper, *Undivided: Closing the Faith-Life Gap* (IVP, 2013).

7

Sex

According to an exclusive poll from *The Sunday Times*, three-quarters of British parents believe that their children will lose their virginity at the age of sixteen or younger, and most allow their teenage children to have sex in their homes. We live in a porn-crazy culture. Young people are inundated with sexual imagery. The single largest group of internet porn customers is twelve- to seventeen-year-olds, while one in three ten-year-olds has seen pornography on the internet, according to a study by Safety Net, a campaign to protect children online. Some 81% of fourteen- to sixteen-year-olds regularly look at explicit photographs and footage on their home computers, with thirteen to fourteen being the peak age at which boys access porn for the first time.[1]

This is evidence of a total cultural revolution which has taken place in my lifetime. And it appears that this dramatic change will continue. The new guidelines issued by the Brook advice service offer a new 'traffic-light' system where types of sexualized behaviour in children are codified. This is so that parents and other carers will know what is normal, and what isn't and should therefore cause concern. Looking at pornography from the age of thirteen is given a green light. Taking a naked or sexually provocative image of yourself or others, or exposing oneself, is given an amber light. You will be pleased to know that sexual degradation and exploitative behaviour, sex with family members or with animals or in exchange for money is given a red light! The Brook is considered a very liberal group, and this advice has caused consternation – but for how long will this be the case?

How is this cultural revolution impacting upon Christian opinion? Christian apologist and evangelist Josh McDowell introduces us to a young woman whom he describes as 'a typical sixteen-year-old Christian from a solid youth group'. He asks her, 'Is it wrong to engage in premarital sex?' 'Well, I believe it's wrong for me,' she responds. McDowell probes further, 'But do you believe the Bible teaches that premarital sex is wrong for everyone?'

'Amber's eyes shift back and forth as she weighs her answer. "Well," she begins slowly, "I know it's wrong for me and I have chosen not to have sex until I'm married, but I don't think I can judge other people on what they do." '[2]

The Maker's instructions

If Jesus is Lord, then this means that whatever cultural changes are taking place, there are absolutes that govern the behaviour of all God's people at all times. When it comes to our sexual behaviour, Paul does not give us his own opinion, but 'instructions . . . by the authority of the Lord Jesus' (1 Thessalonians 4:2). The word translated 'instructions' is a strong one, which in Paul's day would have been used as a military command or a court order. However counter-cultural it may be, if we're going to be disciples of Jesus, it's not a question of 'doing what seems right at the time' or 'doing what seems natural', but of obedience to the clear and definite instruction which the Lord Jesus has given us.

What exactly are these instructions? We will discover them as we look at the verses that follow, but first it is vital to recognize the positive context in which they are given: 'It is God's will that you should be sanctified' (1 Thessalonians 4:3). This means that God wants us to live pure lives, and in the context that means a life of sexual purity.

A friend of mine was having difficulty in her marriage, particularly in the sexual area. She went to see a counsellor who was not a professing Christian. As she explained the issues to her, it wasn't long before the counsellor was asking, 'Excuse me, but are you a born-again Christian?' When she made it clear that she was, the counsellor continued, 'I'm not surprised. I find that so many who come to me are, and they get totally hung up in the area of sex.'

Joyce Huggett was writing a book on relationships while living in Cyprus. She describes how one day she was in the bath when an earthquake occurred. As she ran out of the bathroom, the thought came to her mind: 'Jesus has come – he's returned!' She continues, 'The initial excitement evaporated as I looked down on my naked body. Oh no! He can't choose *this* minute. I'm naked. And I'm dripping wet.'[3] The lesson she learned was that although she had been speaking to audiences for years about what the Bible says about sex, telling thousands to accept their bodies and their sexuality as God-given gifts, she had not reached that position of maturity herself.

Somehow we've contrived to make this beautiful gift from our generous Father an issue of embarrassment, which we don't like to talk about, and when we do, it leaves us feeling slightly dirty. The Bible has a great deal to say about our sexual behaviour, but how often do you hear the subject clearly and practically taught in our churches? The first time that I mentioned masturbation in my own church, I think people thought the walls would fall down, but of course, it's one of the most common, intense sexual issues that we have to deal with.

Do you believe that Jesus was sexually tempted? If you don't, then you're saying that he had every human emotion except probably the greatest one of all. He was hungry, thirsty, tired, but never touched by sexual desire! The truth is that he 'has been tempted in every way, just as we are – yet he did not sin' (Hebrews 4:15).

What comes to your mind when you think of living a holy life? Is it stained-glass windows and monasteries? Possibly it's not that extreme, but I wonder if you are thinking of something completely different, of a truly exciting, fulfilling life? Do you admire the life of Jesus? Do you believe that to live as he lived is truly to live? It certainly seems that the people around Jesus found his life to be extremely attractive. I'm sure that he was the most interesting, engaging, fascinating, stimulating human being who ever lived. He lived a holy life and made it clear that such a life was his desire for his followers too. As we saw earlier, he also said, 'I have come that they [his followers] may have life, and have it to the full' (John 10:10). This was in contrast to 'the thief' who 'comes only to steal and kill and destroy'. Satan's great lie is that his way opens the door to true satisfaction, and that it's God who is

Satan is the thief and the killer, and it is God who is the generous giver who wants his followers to live life to the full.

the killjoy. The reality is that Satan is the thief and the killer, and it is God who is the generous giver who wants his followers to live life to the full. God's will for us is our sanctification, that we should live holy lives, lives that please God.

Believing the lie

Leadership magazine commissioned a poll of 1,000 pastors. It indicated that 12% of them had committed adultery while in ministry, that is, one out of eight pastors, and 23% had done something they considered to be sexually inappropriate.[4]

Christianity Today magazine surveyed 1,000 of its subscribers who were not pastors, and 23% said they had had extramarital intercourse, with 45% indicating that they had done something they themselves had deemed sexually inappropriate. That is, one in four Christian men who are unfaithful, and almost 50% who have behaved in a way they themselves consider inappropriate.[5]

I wish I didn't have to say this, but I'm afraid that it is an all-too-common experience to sit in my office with a weeping Christian who has believed Satan's lie and is paying the consequences. Often that lie has been fed to them in this area of sex, an area where the thief really does like to steal from us. God, through the gift of sex, has given such potential for pleasure and satisfaction. The thief hates the very thought of the people of God having such enjoyment, and of God having such joy in their enjoyment, so he will steal that joy, kill that pleasure and turn this beautiful gift into a total nightmare. The strategy of the thief is to suggest that what God has said is the way to sexual fulfilment just is not the way: 'Why wait until marriage?' he will insinuate. 'It can't possibly do any harm, especially if we are already engaged. That's the proof of our commitment and what possible difference can one further piece of paper make?'

'I haven't gone looking for this. The emotion is just overwhelming, and I can't help myself.' These are the words of a married man who has made the decision to be unfaithful to his partner. We talk ourselves into the move that steals and kills. It steals from your wife or husband, from your children, and often those affected will say later, 'Something died within me that day.'

G. K. Chesterton wrote,

> All healthy men [and I would add women] ancient and modern, Eastern and Western, know that there is a certain fury in sex that we cannot afford to inflame, and that a certain mystery and awe must ever surround it if we are to remain sane.[6]

That is so true. This wonderful gift from God has a certain fury, and without appropriate discipline, it will burn and destroy.

'D' is for discipline

This takes us back to 1 Thessalonians 4:3, quoted earlier in the chapter. So, after setting the positive context, Paul immediately moves to the need for discipline, not because sex is bad, but because it's so good and so powerful that the potential for destruction is just as great as the potential for satisfaction. Sitting behind the wheel of a Ferrari, there are two possible outcomes for me – to have a great experience or to destroy myself, and possibly many others, in a moment – and one could easily lead to the other.

So what discipline is required to ensure that the gift of sex is satisfying rather than destructive? Paul asked the Thessalonians to do two things: 'avoid sexual immorality' and 'learn to control your own body' (1 Thessalonians 4:3–4). The word translated 'sexual immorality' means every kind of illicit sexual intercourse. For the Christian who wants to obey God, that can mean only one thing. The only sexual intercourse that God planned for us, and which, therefore, will be truly satisfying, is with our marriage partner. No exceptions, no special cases, no excuses!

Of course, some might say that this is impossible in the twenty-first century. Surely it sets the bar too high. We've noted the cultural trend, and this is so counter-cultural. In the UK today, fewer than 1% of men and women have their first experience of sex with someone they are married or engaged to. Isn't this an outdated idea that can no longer be valid?

The Scriptures are valid for all people, in all cultures, at all times.

We need to appreciate two things: God did not put any time limit on these commands. The Scriptures are valid for all people, in all cultures, at all times. The people in Thessalonica to whom Paul was writing were living in a highly promiscuous culture like ours: 'The cities of Greece, Asia Minor and Egypt had become centres of the wildest corruption. There has probably never been a period when vice was more extravagant or uncontrolled than it was under the Caesars.'[7] Prior to their conversions, immorality had probably played a part in the religious practices of many of these Thessalonian believers. If we think that living counter-culturally today is a huge challenge, it was no less a challenge for them then.

So how can we live, totally avoiding sexual immorality? In a nutshell, we must 'learn to control our own bodies'. In the context, this can only mean our bodily or sexual desires. That is the challenge. We must learn to control one of the most powerful passions most of us will ever experience.

And after giving this instruction, Paul writes, 'Anyone who rejects this instruction does not reject a human being but God, the very God who gives you his Holy Spirit' (1 Thessalonians 4:8). This shows how serious it is to take sexual sin lightly. Such sin may offend other people, but supremely it is an offence to God. To fail to take sexual sin seriously is to fail to take God seriously, and particularly this wonderful gift that he has given us which we looked at in chapter 5: the gift of his Holy Spirit.

> Flee from sexual immorality. All other sins a person commits are outside the body, but whoever sins sexually, sins against their own body. Do you not know that your bodies are temples of the Holy Spirit, who is in you, whom you have received from God? You are not your own; you were bought at a price. Therefore honour God with your bodies.
> (1 Corinthians 6:18–20)

In sexual sin we violate the sacredness of our bodies which are now the temples of God's Spirit.

The eye, the mind and the power of the Spirit

I'm so grateful that Paul mentions the Holy Spirit as he explains God's commands to the Thessalonians. For without his powerful enabling, I cannot live this life of purity. A power greater than my powerful sexual desire is required, and thank God, that power is there and available for us: the power of God, the Holy Spirit. And we are called to cooperate with God the Holy Spirit, if we are to live in purity. It's not just a question of turning on the power when we get into difficulty. We must obey the Holy Spirit and the Word that the Holy Spirit inspired.

Discipline must begin with the eye and the mind. However efficient the software safeguards we install, they will never be sufficient. It's going to take daily dogged determination in the power of the Holy Spirit to stay clean in your mind and heart if this is an issue you grapple with. There is no sexual failure that did not begin with an undisciplined eye and continue with an undisciplined mind. Today, sadly, that indiscipline often finds expression in spending time on internet pornography sites. At the time of writing, I'm told that 12% of all sites are now of this nature, and a quarter of all internet search engines will locate one of those sites. In some churches, surveys have shown that a staggering one in two people are spending time on these sites. It seems this problem has reached epidemic proportions. If we're serious about discipline in this area, then we will build into our lives and our hardware safeguards and accountability arrangements. I have a colleague who travels extensively and finds himself particularly vulnerable to sexual failure because of this. He informs me of his travel schedule in advance and invites me to telephone him to ask him the hard questions about how he has been doing. Simple systems and safeguards can be installed on our computers which can give some help if online pornography is something you battle with.

Long before the internet era we see a clear example of how sexual failure happens, and how it can be avoided, in the story of King David and Bathsheba. King David had been leading his troops out in battle for years. On this occasion, he stays at home and sends out his troops under the leadership of Joab. Some criticize David for that, but surely even the king needs a break! Satan, however, is different. He doesn't seem to need a break and certainly never seems to take one.

David can't sleep. Is this the great leader concerned for his men? He takes a walk on the palace roof, and from there he sees a beautiful woman, Bathsheba, bathing. Should we be critical of Bathsheba for the place she chooses? There is

David's first opportunity. He can immediately walk back into his palace, but I don't think he did. He stayed and he looked. It went beyond: 'What a beautiful woman!' That powerful sexual drive was kicking in. David finally goes back inside the palace, but now his thoughts are raging. 'I'll send someone to find out who she is,' he decides. This is his second grave error. He has an opportunity to walk away, but the 'fury' is now burning, and unless he takes action soon, it's going to hurt him and others.

The servant returns: 'She is Bathsheba, the daughter of Eliam and the wife of Uriah the Hittite' (2 Samuel 11:3). She's a married woman. So will he walk away now? No, the way of escape was there on more than one occasion, but he didn't take it. Instead, he takes the route that will lead to devastation for Bathsheba and her husband Uriah, and permanent scarring for David himself.

The Psalms help us to understand some of the emotions of this incident. It was only after a baby was born from this adulterous act that David repented when confronted by Nathan. For at least nine months he was living with un-confessed sin:

> When I kept silent,
>   my bones wasted away
>   through my groaning all day long.
> For day and night
>   your hand was heavy on me;
> my strength was sapped
>   as in the heat of summer.
> (Psalm 32:3–4)

Some interpreters suggest that David wrote these words during that nine-month period. After he finally confesses his sin, he cries out to God, 'Restore to me the joy of your salvation' (Psalm 51:12).

The thief has been at work, robbing David of his strength, his joy. David crossed the line when he sent for Bathsheba.

In 1 Thessalonians 4:6 Paul says, '[In this matter] no one should wrong or take advantage of a brother or sister.' John Stott writes, 'The first verb has the force of crossing a boundary – here, of course, a forbidden boundary, and hence trespassing (sexually) on territory which is not your own – while the second verb is the desire to possess more than one should in any area of life.'[8] If someone tells you they have never been drawn to that line, check their pulse! We have all been there, but God is there with us, and we do not need to cross that line. The desire is not uncontrollable: that is a devilish suggestion. By the power of the Holy Spirit, we can live in purity, even in our twenty-first-century culture. We can look away; we can walk away in the power of the Holy Spirit.

> *By the power of the Holy Spirit, we can live in purity, even in our twenty-first-century culture.*

Grace: the way back

Some of you are feeling that this is all irrelevant because you have already failed. The thief loves to say that what you have lost, you have lost forever. But he's lying again, and not surprisingly, as he is 'the father of lies' (John 8:44). David's joy and strength were restored after his repentance. Yes, there was ongoing damage in his life, but he knew the power of the Holy Spirit again, and he knew what it was to be useful once more in the service of God. Sexual sin can have grave consequences for others and ourselves, but don't let anyone suggest to you that it's the unforgivable sin.

Some, after sexual sin, know that they are forgiven. Yes, they know the doctrine of forgiveness in their heads, but they find it very difficult to accept the reality emotionally. God may have forgiven them, but can they forgive themselves? I spoke to a young man who had failed in this area, and he said, 'I knew God loved me, but I didn't think he liked me.' He certainly didn't like himself. Gradually, however, he saw that he had been imposing an identity on himself: 'I am a moral failure.' Through counselling, he began to realize that what he had done was not who he was. What he had done had been brought to the cross, and the blood of Christ had atoned for it, along with all his other sins. He was, and he is now, a son of God. He knew moral failure, but God no longer sees that failure. His sins have been hurled 'into the depths of the sea' (Micah 7:19). He is a child of God: that is his identity, and God loves and likes his children.

Singleness: a calling

Another lie of the enemy is that there can be no true life without a sexual relationship. In this sexualized age we need to appreciate that the person who modelled perfect humanity for us, the Lord Jesus Christ, was a single man who lived a sexually celibate life. I know many Christians who struggle with singleness, but I also know many who struggle within marriage. The Scriptures are very clear that singleness must not be seen as some kind of disorder. Paul wrote of some of the advantages of being single, actually describing singleness as a charismatic gift (1 Corinthians 7:7). I am a very happily married man, so all I feel qualified to say is that I am convinced that singleness and marriage are both callings of God, with their own particular joys and sorrows, and that God gives sufficient grace for both.

The beautiful gift of sex has been soiled. The consequences of that are visible all around us. Our culture prides itself on its sexual freedom, but the consequences of this so-called 'freedom' are broken homes, broken lives and broken bodies. We need to come back to our Maker's instructions where we will find real freedom.

Questions

1. 'There is a certain fury in sex.' Is there any area of your life where you are currently playing with fire?
2. 'There is no sexual failure that did not begin with an undisciplined eye and continue with an undisciplined mind.' Think about that statement, asking yourself whether there are any actions you need to take in the light of it.

Books

Tim Chester, *Captured by a Better Vision: Living Porn-Free* (IVP, 2010).

Vaughan Roberts, *Battles Christians Face: Tackling Big Issues with Confidence* (Authentic, 2007).

Helen Thorne, *Purity Is Possible: How to Live Free of the Fantasy Trap* (The Good Book Company, 2014).

Paul David Tripp, *Sex and Money: Empty Pleasures, Satisfying Grace* (IVP, 2013).

8

Money

Almost all my working life I have lived 'by faith'. This is the in-house Christian language meaning that I haven't had a regular wage but have looked to God and his people to meet my family's needs. I've come to see that it's a quite silly expression, because surely every Christian lives in this way – dependent upon God? As I've got to know some business people and single parents, to give just two examples, their 'by-faith' life has been just as real as mine.

The lifestyle has been thrilling. It has often been a roller coaster, but by God's grace, the wheels have never come off the waggon. A very real experience of Jehovah Jireh: God our Provider. Sometimes the timing of God's provision has been something for the New Atheists to chew over. One morning a year or two ago, for example, I was shocked to receive through the post a tax bill that I was not expecting. Later that morning an envelope was pushed through my door containing a cheque for exactly the amount of the tax bill. It came from the estate of a man with whom I had had a major policy disagreement in the charity which we together advised. I thought I had deeply offended him, but clearly he was a man of grace!

Money is a big issue for Christians today. As a means of exchange, it is in itself neutral, a means of payment necessary to make the world go round. But the accumulation of it has become much more than that. Indeed, many people view their self-worth on the basis of how much of it they possess, while for others it is a determining issue in choosing their friends. Those who can splash the cash are envied. For those with enough purchasing power, consumerism has become a form of freedom: 'I can do whatever I want to do.' Those without purchasing power can easily feel bound and restricted, and resentment of the 'haves' can quickly build up.

Society today is even defined by money. We live in 'a materialistic society, a consumer age'. Consumerism, it is argued, is the religion of the twenty-first century: the shopping mall is now the place of worship for many on a Sunday morning. We used to consume to live, but now it seems we live to consume.

Andrew Walker, Emeritus Professor of Theology, Culture and Education at King's College, London, comments thus:

> Beginning in the United States, and heralded in the 1940s by Henry Ford, consumerism has become the dominant cultural force of the last half of the [twentieth] century . . . After the Second World War, rising standards of living, full employment, technological advance and innovative marketing spearheaded the American revolution that has led to its cultural dominance and imitation ever since.[1]

The global financial crisis in the early part of this century caused some to question this culture, but it is amazing how quickly we forget, and today not much seems to have changed. We live in constant danger of being deceived by the architects and promoters of this culture. The ability to supply goods in our world far outstrips the real need for such goods. The only way to keep the consumer show on the road is to sell us what we don't need, and to make sure that many of the things sold wear out very quickly. The constant message of the marketer is: 'You must have this; life is really unimaginable without it.' Our flexible friend, the credit card, stands by so that we can have, even when we don't have.

As Christian disciples, we are on a journey with someone who certainly would not have been duped by this message. He was very clear: 'Life does not consist in an abundance of possessions' (Luke 12:15). Jesus was very interested in wealth; he was interested in his followers accumulating it. But it was a very different kind of wealth:

> Do not store up for yourselves treasures on earth, where moths and vermin destroy, and where thieves break in and steal. But store up for yourselves treasures in heaven, where moths and vermin do not destroy, and where thieves do not break in and steal.
> (Matthew 6:19–20)

A vital statement follows in the next verse which should lead us all to self-examination: 'For where your treasure is, there your heart will be also.'

It's not difficult to check your spiritual health. Where is your heart? What attracts your interest and your time? Is it the things of this world, the drive to possess things now, or am I more interested in, and therefore spend more time thinking and dreaming about, my eternal reward and treasure?

The cultural pressure to throw yourself into this consumer thinking is immense and constant. How then should a follower of Jesus live in today's society?

Generosity

We are called to be 'followers of God', the God who 'so loved the world that he gave his one and only Son' (John 3:16). Our God is a giver, not a hoarder, and he gives extravagantly!

I remember a period when our children were growing up, and money was in short supply. When they came asking for things, I tried to respond, but I was a real 'bean counter', and I gave them only what they needed, that is, the bare minimum! But that is not the way God gives. Flick back to the beginning of the Old Testament: 'The LORD God made all kinds of trees grow out of the ground – trees that were pleasing to the eye and good for food' (Genesis 2:9). His creation was not the bare minimum. He didn't give just enough to eat. Some of what he made was 'pleasing to the eye', just there for us to enjoy.

Move through the Old Testament a little way and you will see that the land he gave to his people, Israel, was a land 'flowing with milk and honey' (Numbers 14:8). And as we have already noted from the Gospels, Jesus came to give us abundant life, life to be lived to the full (John 10:10). When Jesus saves a person, he gives him or her life in the fullest sense – life of the highest quality imaginable. When you read of eternal life, yes, it is certainly about length. Jesus said, 'Whoever lives by believing in me will never die' (John 11:26). But it is also about the *quality* of our lives today.

But in a way that baffles belief, this call to generosity has been hijacked by some and become part of what we might call 'Christian consumerism'. 'Give and you will get' is the message of the proponents of the prosperity gospel. And, sadly, it's a message proclaimed with greatest success in the poorest parts of the world. It is a complete capitulation to our consumer culture. I am sure you have not been duped by this utter heresy, but there is a parallel danger – that we find ourselves slipping into entitlement thinking: 'If I am walking with God, then things should go reasonably well.' Loss of a job, a period of ill health, and faith questions are quickly triggered within us. God is not a slot machine, and we must trust him when his purposes are greater and wiser than ours.

The disciple of Jesus should be marked by generosity – the giving of money, time and abilities for the glory of God and the good of people, and for no other motive.

Contentment

The apostle Paul would have been a marketer's nightmare. One sentence that he wrote to the Philippian church would have sent the leaders of this consumer age scurrying into emergency committee meetings: 'I have learned to be content whatever the circumstances' (Philippians 4:11). Contentment whatever the circumstances? What happens to the consumer dream if we find contentment in what we have and reject the idea that we must have 'the next thing'?

I have a hero who is neither a missionary nor a vicar! He's a businessman, and a very successful one at that. I've known him for many years, and during those years his personal income has increased significantly as his companies have developed. Yet his lifestyle hardly seems to have changed. He lives in the same house as when his business was small. It's a pleasant home, and his lifestyle certainly includes some things that many would consider luxuries. What has impressed me is that his lifestyle decisions have not been income determined.

I have rarely witnessed anyone living like this. The message of the consumer age is: 'If you have it, it's yours to spend, and to truly live, you must go on spending.' This man certainly has it, but spends only a very moderate amount on himself. The rest is given to a number of Christian ministries, many of which would probably not survive without his generosity.

Sacrifice

As we saw in chapter 4, we are walking the discipleship road with the man who gave everything for us: 'I lay down my life for the sheep' (John 10:15). The giving heart of God is seen in Paul's words to the church at Rome: 'He who did not spare his own Son, but gave him up for us all – how will he not also, along with him, graciously give us all things?' (Romans 8:32). The gift of Jesus is so huge, it's indescribable (2 Corinthians 9:15). Speaking to his disciples about self-denial, Jesus is clear that the only way to save your life is to give it away (Matthew 16:25). He said that to follow him meant giving up everything (Luke 14:33). On both of these occasions Jesus was not just referring to money, but we fool ourselves if we think money never crossed his mind as he made those statements.

> *The gift of Jesus is so huge, it's indescribable.*

So the consumer age says, 'It's yours – accumulate it, spend it as you choose, indulge yourself – because you're worth it!' But for the Christian disciple, it's not all about me. As we've seen, one of the fundamental understandings of discipleship is: 'I am a steward.' God created me, and then through Christ redeemed me. My life is his. Everything I am and have is his. This is exactly what the early disciples meant when they developed the first creed of the Christian church: 'Jesus Christ is Lord.'

All that I have is his; he gives it to me on trust; I am to use everything for his glory. This does not mean that I cannot enjoy what God gives me. We looked earlier at heresies suggesting that in some way, physical, material things are evil or at least second best. This kind of false teaching appeared in the earliest days of the church (1 Timothy 4:2–5).

What it comes down to is really our attitude. It is attitude that Paul concentrates on when he writes to the rich:

> Command those who are rich in this present world not to be arrogant nor to put their hope in wealth, which is so uncertain, but to put their hope in God, who richly provides us with everything for our enjoyment. Command them to do good, to be rich in good deeds, and to be generous and willing to share. In this way they will lay up treasure for themselves as a firm foundation for the coming age, so that they may take hold of the life that is truly life.
> (1 Timothy 6:17–19)

So an open-handedness and a healthy detachment from wealth should characterize the Christian disciple: 'Yes, I work hard, but I know I'm only where I am through God's faithfulness. Everything I have is ultimately his. I want to use it wisely and generously for his glory. I can give sacrificially because I trust him, the great Provider, and the great example of sacrificial giving. He is no man's debtor.'

Trusting in what?

Like me, many of you reading this book will be wealthy in global terms. If you're driving a car or living in a two- or three-bedroomed house, then you're probably among the wealthiest 10% in our world. The danger then is that I begin to trust in what I have: 'The job looks secure, and income seems guaranteed; I've got the mortgage and I think I can handle the payments; I've even got some savings stashed away if there are rainy days ahead.' That thinking is not wrong, and indeed, it may well point to good planning. But if we're not careful, without realizing it, we begin to trust in all of this. We think we have achieved it all by our own effort and intelligence. Thankfulness to God goes out of the window. Then we think that with continued good planning, the good times will be secure. Reliance on God now goes out of the window. We become self-sufficient rather than God-dependent. Our effort becomes the basis of trust, rather than our faith in God.

There are warning signs that you can look out for which indicate that you are moving from being God-dependent to self-sufficient. One of these signs that Paul writes about here is arrogance or pride:

> Command those who are rich in this present world not to be arrogant nor to put their hope in wealth, which is so uncertain, but to put their hope in God, who richly provides us with everything for our enjoyment.
> (1 Timothy 6:17).

You begin to take yourself or your wealth too seriously. The richer you become, the greater the danger. As we've seen, the world looks up to those who are doing well materially. If we're not careful, we can begin to believe the illusion that 'things' are really what life is all about, and therefore we're not doing so badly! To trust in something which is 'so uncertain' is so foolish, especially when our hope can be in God, the great faithful Provider.

Sharing or sparing?

When Paul wrote these words to Timothy, the church congregations were very mixed economically. We know that many were slaves, and there were poor widows in the congregations, but some well-heeled people had also come to faith. In such a situation the good works expected of every disciple would require the rich to be 'generous and willing to share' (1 Timothy 6:18). They'd been blessed in order to be a blessing. Paul makes this very clear when he's collecting from Christian churches after a time of famine which had left the Christians in Jerusalem in great need:

> Our desire is not that others might be relieved while you are hard pressed, but that there might be equality. At the present time your plenty will supply what they need, so that in turn their plenty will supply what you need. The goal is equality, as it is written: 'The one who gathered much did not have too much, and the one who gathered little did not have too little.' (2 Corinthians 8:13–15)

For those of us who are wealthy, it is good to recognize that if we use our material blessings well, then we will be spiritually blessed. In this way, Paul writes, the rich will 'lay up treasure for themselves as a firm foundation for the coming age, so that they may take hold of the life that is truly life' (1 Timothy 6:19). We actually have a choice. Paul, in his fundraising letter to the Corinthian church (2 Corinthians 8 – 9), writes, 'Remember this: whoever sows sparingly will also reap sparingly, and whoever sows generously will also reap generously' (2 Corinthians 9:6). The context of this statement is money. So, if you want to be blessed – think big; then give – big!

Plan ahead

If we're going to get really serious about this, then some thinking and planning are essential.

First, plan a giving system. Don't just give emotionally when you see or hear of a particular need. Paul's advice to the Corinthians was:

> On the first day of every week, each one of you should set aside a sum of money in keeping with your income, saving it up, so that when I come [to receive the money for the famine victims in Jerusalem] no collections will have to be made.
> (1 Corinthians 16:2).

I have a vivid memory from childhood of my dad opening his wage packet each week. There were two tins in the cupboard: one was known as 'The Lord's tin', and the other was the holiday tin. The first action was to put a percentage into the Lord's tin and then a percentage into the holiday tin. In times of hardship, money could be borrowed from the holiday tin, but never from the Lord's tin!

Notice how Paul writes that what we 'set aside' should be 'in keeping with [our] income'. So, giving will change. As our income increases or decreases, our giving will change too. I think we need to plan that in advance. Couples need to discuss it. Are we going to give a percentage of everything received? Are we going to give a percentage of everything received up to a certain amount, and then give everything beyond that amount?

This is a very personal decision, but a great thing to discuss with spouses, families, and other Christians, particularly those with whom you have an accountability relationship.

Consider the following biblical principles as you plan your giving. It should be:

1. a joyful aspect of your Christian discipleship (2 Corinthians 9:7).
2. sacrificial. There is a great principle for life found in 2 Samuel 24:22–24. In obedience to Gad the prophet, David goes to Araunah the Jebusite to build an altar to the Lord on his threshing floor. David tells Araunah that he wants to buy his threshing floor to do this. Araunah insists, 'Let my lord the king take whatever he wishes and offer it up.' He also offers his oxen for the sacrifice and all the instruments David would require. David's response is: 'No, I insist on paying you for it. I will not sacrifice to the LORD my God burnt offerings that cost me nothing.'
3. in proportion to your income (1 Corinthians 16:2).
4. intentional (1 Corinthians 16:2).

In his book *Joy in Ministry*, Michael Duduit tells the story of J. C. Stribling and the 1929 stock market crash in America. Prior to the Great Depression, Stribling was a wealthy Texas rancher. He owned a great deal of land, thousands of head of cattle and a fortune in stocks and bonds. During this time he gave $150,000 to build a girls' dormitory on the campus of Mary Harding-Baylor College, a Baptist college in Texas.

Then came the Depression. He was reduced to virtual poverty. One day in 1933 a pastor came to the side of Stribling's old run-down Ford and spoke to Stribling and his wife. Pastor Brandon explained that he had just returned from driving a group of girls to enrol in the college. He had spent the night there, and now wanted to thank Mr Stribling for his gift. Stribling was silent for a few moments as his eyes filled with tears. Then he spoke, 'That was all we saved out of a mighty fortune. It was what we gave that we were able to keep forever.'

> 'It was what we gave that we were able to keep forever . . . I wish I had given more.'

Then he added this challenge: 'Preacher, tell people to give all they can to the kingdom of God while they have it. I wish I had given more.'[2]

Jesus said,

Do not store up for yourselves treasures on earth, where moths and vermin destroy, and where thieves break in and steal. But store up for yourselves treasures in heaven, where moths and vermin do not destroy, and where thieves do not break in and steal. For where your treasure is, there your heart will be also. (Matthew 6:19–21)

Questions

1. Are we going to let consumerism shape our core values, or are we going to insist that our Christian perspective must shape our consumption?
2. 'It was what we were able to give away that we were able to keep forever.' Think about that statement. Do you have a giving plan? If not, don't you need one? If you have one already, do you need to review it?

Books

Ash Carter, *The Money Mentor: Getting to Grips with Your Finances* (IVP, 2010).

9

Time

The great time robbery

One of the biggest parenting challenges today, it seems, is controlling 'screen time': the television, of course, but also the computer screen, iPhone, tablet or whatever gadget is to hand.

The danger is that, without careful oversight from parents, children will spend a significant part of their lives in front of a screen. The whole thing has become like a drug: if the smartphone gets lost, you can almost see physical symptoms of distress developing. There are different estimates of the average number of hours children spend in front of a screen. Most surveys conclude that it is somewhere between four and seven hours daily. That's between twenty-eight and forty hours each week, about as much time in front of a screen as adults are spending at work. Some of this screen time can, of course, be useful and educational, but a lot of it is not. Some of it is just 'filling time' and some positively harmful.

And this is not just an issue for children. I know that if I don't take active steps to control my iPhone, it will control me as I respond to its every bleep. It's part of a much bigger issue and one that is vital to discipleship. Writing to the Ephesians, Paul states, 'Be very careful, then, how you live – not as unwise but as wise' (5:15). The first evidence that we are living wisely will be seen in our use of time: 'making the most of every opportunity, because the days are evil' (verse 16). The Authorized Version translates the verb in verse 16 as 'redeeming the time . . .'. Just as the slave was redeemed, bought back from the master, so too we must discipline ourselves to buy back time from being wasted. In these 'evil days', the natural tendency will be to waste time. Without deliberate action on our part, this will happen. 'Don't live carelessly, unthinkingly. Make sure you understand what the Master wants' is *The Message* paraphrase of Ephesians 5:17. Carelessness in our use of time is a great danger: there are so many distractions, things to watch, read, play, listen to. Many are not evil in themselves, but they will distract you. Those goals you felt you needed to achieve at the beginning of the day, and really wanted to get to, are not achieved. Instead, you will find yourself thinking, 'I wonder where that day went to?' The truth is that it didn't go anywhere. It was all there, all twenty-four hours of it. You just missed big chunks of it!

When I was much younger, television was straightforward. There were four channels, and often it was quickly clear that there wasn't anything particularly worth watching. But today there are so many channels available that you can always find something which you can convince yourself is 'worth' watching.

A gift to treasure

Time is a precious gift that must never be taken for granted. The Roman philosopher Seneca observed, 'We are always complaining that our days are few but acting as if they would never end.' The apostle James made a parallel point:

> Now listen, you who say, 'Today or tomorrow we will go to this or that city, spend a year there, carry on business and make money.' Why, you do not even know what will happen tomorrow. What is your life? You are a mist that appears for a little while and then vanishes. Instead, you ought to say, 'If it is the Lord's will, we will live and do this or that.' As it is, you boast in your arrogant schemes. All such boasting is evil. If anyone, then, knows the good they ought to do and doesn't do it, it is sin for them.
> (James 4:13–17)

I remember when three score years and ten seemed to me like an eternity. Today it feels like a very short time. Moses appreciated just how quickly those years fly by:

> Our days may come to seventy years,
>   or eighty, if our strength endures;
> yet the best of them are but trouble and sorrow,
>   for they quickly pass, and we fly away.
> (Psalm 90:10)

The Puritan preacher, Robert Wilkinson, puts this seventy-year time-span into perspective: 'Take out the first ten years for infancy and childhood . . . then take a third part of your life as sleep, take away those days before you came to know Christ and any days when you have not walked closely with him and what remains is very little.' No wonder Moses prays,

> Teach us to number our days,
>   that we may gain a heart of wisdom.
> (verse 12)

He is asking God to teach him to live in the light of the brevity of life, to number or calculate the time he has remaining. Of course, none of us knows that time. As believers in the second coming of Christ, we know that our future plans can be disrupted at any moment.

First things first

There are certain things in life which are just more important than others. This is especially true for the follower of Christ. Jesus said, 'Seek first his kingdom and his righteousness, and all these things will be given to you as well' (Matthew 6:33). The interest of our King and his kingdom must take priority.

We're called to be good citizens wherever we live. Peter exhorts us to submit for the Lord's sake to every authority instituted among men, and to honour our leaders (1 Peter 2:13, 17). We are to make a positive contribution wherever we are, and have a good testimony: 'Live such good lives among the pagans that, though they accuse you of doing wrong, they may see your good deeds and glorify God on the day he visits us' (verse 12). Yet we are 'foreigners and exiles' in the world (verse 11), called to live by the principles and values of 'the age to come' right in the middle of this present age, where the call is to give our time, energy and talents to develop those things that the spirit of this age values.

Jesus' call is to give priority to those things that he values. Jesus says that if we do prioritize them this way, 'All these things will be given to [us], as well.' 'These things' are just those things that so many give so much time and attention to: living longer, eating and drinking, our clothes, and so forth. Jesus is not saying not to give time to these things, rather not to worry about them, and they should never be given top priority.

The pressure is on to do the normal things that friends and neighbours do. We're expected to look after ourselves, care for our homes, dress appropriately and put the car through the car wash. As disciples of Christ, we should certainly do these things, and society expects it. But who is going to notice and express any concern if we are inconsistent in our prayer lives or our Bible reading? Who is going to notice if we go through yet another week without looking for opportunities to witness to our Saviour? The danger is that 'these things' take priority because of society's expectations, and 'his kingdom' issues are very much in second place.

Have you ever considered analysing where your time goes? Start with a day. Divide your working time into hours and chart the main ways in which your time is used. Admittedly, it may be difficult, because knowing you're going to do this may affect the way you choose to spend your day!

Alc is not the only holic

I have found that I regularly need to take steps to slow down in order to spend my time well. Life now moves at such a pace, that reflection time will need to be scheduled or it's unlikely to happen. We're surrounded by bleeps and buzzers and bells. We need to get away from it all on a regular basis just to think! I try to do this in the morning before the real busyness of the day begins. Years ago, that would have been the worst time, with young children making their rightful demands on us in those early hours. I consciously try to slow down and relax in God's presence to discover the priorities of my day when I'm in that place before him.

The distinction Gordon MacDonald makes in his book, *Ordering Your Private World*, is one that I've found helpful.[1] He differentiates between the called and the driven person. Sadly, for many years I was a driven person. Driven by my own ego and the expectations I thought others had of me. I was very busy; I accepted almost any ministry opportunity that came my way, as long as it would somehow fit into the diary. It felt good. I was needed, wanted and applauded, but I wasn't seeking first God's kingdom. If anything, I was seeking first my kingdom. It is so easy when you are serving Christ to rationalize an over-busy life.

I will never forget talking with a wonderful couple who served God in India for many years. They had three children in the early years of their marriage. The husband's work in India involved visiting missionary teams all over the country. He was constantly away from home, often for considerable periods of time. And that home was not easy for his wife and children to live in.

It is so easy when you are serving Christ to rationalize an over-busy life.

It was shared with a team of young male missionaries. But the couple soldiered on for a number of years. In the end, it temporarily broke their health, came close to breaking their marriage and almost led to their backsliding from the faith. As they looked back on that time, they realized they had convinced themselves that this was their calling. It was the price they had to pay to fulfil the ministry they had been given. But do you think that the call to self-sacrifice, which is a definite part of the call to discipleship and ministry, really means the sacrifice of the well-being of others and of ourselves?

It was a vital, wonderful day when God showed me the foolishness of the lifestyle of my early years as an itinerant preacher. A life-changing day when I asked God, 'What contribution do you want me to make to your kingdom? What calling and gifts and capacity have you entrusted to me?' I took a card and wrote down four things I was sure God wanted me to give my time and energy to. Every invitation I have received since then I have sought to respond to in the light of those four priorities. Will my acceptance of that invitation further any of these? Sadly, ego has still won the day far too often, but the difference has been sufficient for it to be life changing. If we are going to respond to Paul's exhortation to redeem the time, we will need to prioritize, and if you are like me, you will need to plan seasons to slow down and reflect in order to prioritize well.

The last thing I want to do through this chapter is to create more workaholics. Surely there are enough of them around already! My teaching ministry has taken me inside many other mission groups, churches and Christian organizations, in addition to Operation Mobilisation. I have spent a lot of time with leaders. A constant subject of conversation across the board is the work-life balance. How do we get this right, between work, family, leisure, church and developing our relationship with God? 'I spend my life juggling and constantly dropping balls,' say some. Most of the stories I hear are of regret and failure. Yes, you are right, it's an area where I too have regularly struggled and often failed. Over the years I've stayed in the homes of hundreds of Christian families when I've been speaking in their churches, and I've heard their stories.

It didn't take me long to understand that this is not just an issue for those working with Christian organizations and churches. The fact that many are getting this wrong is becoming more widely recognized. Richard Branson has told the staff at Virgin's head office that they can go on holiday whenever they like and for as long as they like, provided they have done all their work and their temporary departure doesn't mess anything up. He is recognizing that something has gone wrong with 'the working week'.[2] Longer and longer hours are not leading to greater productivity. Weary workers with fractured home lives, where the division between the working day and private time is ever more blurred, do not translate into greater effectiveness.

I notice a fairly regular pattern. Just at the time when children are growing up, responsibility at work is also ramping up. It can be exciting. More responsibility, more challenges, maybe an extra work-related course or two that you need to take, and the only way is to squeeze it into evenings and weekends. This happens at a period in your life when church is looking to you to take major responsibility. As the children grow, you need a larger property, and the mortgage payments are an extra incentive to 'put in the hours'. The years pass with varying degrees of stress and strain. Then you get into your fifties or maybe sixties, and the excitement about work is beginning to fade. You begin to evaluate as you look back, and look forward to the future. Regret is so often the dominant feeling at that time. What do you regret? 'Oh, I wish I'd spent more time at work!' Really? I don't ever recall hearing that sentiment expressed. It's more like: 'The family suffered', or 'My walk with God has not been what it should be.'

I have no desire to create a false sense of guilt. I'm concerned, as I write, that some of you may already be feeling condemned rather than motivated by what I'm writing. Win and I had two children in the first two years of our marriage. Those early years were survival time. A peaceful, quiet time before the day began? Forget it! If we could sleep at all, we slept! It was a case of grabbing a moment here or there. The priorities of how we spent our time were decided mostly by others, namely our two beautiful babies!

There are seasons in life that require different responses from us. I entered a very different season when I retired from my role as International Director of OM. In the years when I had executive responsibility, my diary was fixed to a certain degree by that. Today it is very different. Yet both periods of my life have required discipline if time was not to be wasted. In those executive years I had to be very disciplined in not allowing my work to overwhelm every other part of my life: devotional, family, rest, social and intellectual. Today it would be possible to allow time to drift away and be wasted. While I believe I'm in a season of life where more rest than in previous seasons is appropriate, it is again a challenge to get the balance right.

Redressing the balance

How then do we get the balance right? The answer isn't easy. Indeed, some may think that I have no right to address the question after a lifetime working with Christian organizations. 'What do you know of the stresses and strains of the "secular" workplace?' some might ask. There is no doubt that it *is* different working within Christian organizations. Stresses and strains may vary, though they are not in my view any less than those in other organizations. In fact, my experience is that it is even more difficult for a Christian working within a church or Christian organization to get the work-life balance right.

Try to make this issue of the work-life balance a topic of conversation. Talk about it with your spouse, and if you have children, why not involve them? It's a real cause of considerable underlying stress in many marriages and families, so isn't it best just to get it out into the open? Put it on the table and talk. Surely this is something that small groups in our churches should be discussing. If you have an accountability group, it should also be a regular topic of discussion there too.

I'm nervous to ask the next questions, but I'm going to be bold. (I don't think you know my address!) If this is causing stress for you and your family, do you truly need to live at the standard that you've chosen? Some of you reading this, I appreciate, may be working morning, noon and night just to survive. I don't want you to be offended by my question. But this is not the case for everyone. You have made a decision to live at a particular level. Would a percentage lifestyle cut be possible? This might take away the need to work at the stress level you are currently at. This is not because work is bad, as we shall see in the next chapter, but it is overwork that I'm concerned about. I read recently of a man and his wife who both worked in the City in London. They did ridiculous hours and had all the trappings of that lifestyle, trappings which included a beautiful home, the latest and best in clothes and cars and, of course, a holiday home. But the trappings also included disappointed and rebellious children, and a marriage that was coming apart at the seams. They made a dramatic decision. They left London, went to live in the country, moved from working seven days a week to four. Do you think they regretted it? They couldn't maintain their previous lifestyle, but the country life was far more satisfying than their London lives. They were fortunate. They had already made a lot of money. They had the kind of job which allowed them to move to a four-day week. Are there changes you could make which might lose you some 'things' but gain even greater ones?

To do this will mean standing against the constant suggestions of our consumer culture. As Dallas Willard writes,

The good life of advertisements is eating a chocolate bar on a sun-kissed beach in paradise. It's being two stone lighter, or looking twenty years younger. It's what you wear, or what you have. It's the holiday of a lifetime, the feel of an expensive luxury car, or a sip of an exclusive brandy. It's owning a dream cottage in the country. This 'good life' is a hotchpotch of hedonism (just do it), escapism (the holiday location always looks better in the brochure) and materialism (shop till you drop).

More money is currently spent on advertising than on education, so in terms of influence, advertising executives are our primary educators. They are successful, and therefore highly paid, teachers. We trust their message – and go out and buy their stuff. Millions of us are working harder, longer hours as we chase the good life.

Back to basics

To what degree are these things an issue for us because we haven't learned the lessons of our earlier chapters? If I live every day in the light of that day, how will it impact my work-life balance? If my 'old self' has been crucified and I've refused the demands of that old self, responding instead to the promptings of the Spirit, what does that do to work-life balance?

Isn't one of the reasons why so many struggle so much in this area that we don't really trust God? Can't we trust him with our financial future? Is our self-worth not so rooted in our position in Christ that we no longer need to exhaust ourselves in our constant craving for human approval?

Surely the Sabbath principle is a bottom line for us. I think one reason why God ordained six days of work and one of rest is just that it's healthy. The Maker of our bodies knows exactly how they should be cared for and how they operate most effectively. I don't think it needs to be rigid. It's possible that a day off could just leave you feeling more stressed, not less. If that's the case, then work that week and take extra time off the next. The Sabbath-day rest doesn't mean a day when you have to do nothing at all! That would leave me totally stressed out! It's a day of change, a change of rhythm and focus. The reason for the Sabbath day in Deuteronomy 5 was that, together, the children of Israel would have the opportunity to remember God's goodness to them in their deliverance from evil: 'Remember that you were slaves in Egypt and that the LORD your God brought you out of there with a mighty hand and an outstretched arm. Therefore the LORD your God has commanded you to observe the Sabbath day' (Deuteronomy 5:15). Isn't it a brilliant practice to enjoy one day each week, when the worship of the Lord, together with his people, can have priority? Achieving the work-life balance may not be easy, but certainly a first vital step will be to build a Sabbath rhythm into our busy and overloaded lives.

Questions

1. Are there changes you could make which might lose you some 'things' but gain greater new things?
2. Do a study of the Sabbath in Scripture. Do you need to change the rhythm of your life in any way as a result?

Books

Kevin DeYoung, *Crazy Busy: A (Mercifully) Short Book about a (Really) Big Problem* (IVP, 2013).
Gordon MacDonald, *Ordering Your Private World* (Highland Books, 2003).

10

Work

For many years I saw work as a necessary evil. It was a distraction from the true calling of a Christian. I went to work to put bread on the table, and if I could do this in less time so that I was freed up to do more 'Christian' work, then that was ideal.

We recognized when looking at the sacred-secular divide earlier how wrong this type of thinking is. Whether you're a minister, a mechanic, a mother or a missionary, the call is absolutely the same: to glorify God in your work. The principle is: 'Whether you eat or drink or whatever you do, do it all for the glory of God' (1 Corinthians 10:31). Our work is to be offered up as an act of worship. Aren't those on the front lines engaging with the world the ordinary Christians in business, industry, the health service, the world of education and the home?

Imitating a worker

God is a worker. Creation is his work. He was creating for

six days, then on the seventh day he rested. Creation needs sustaining, so God goes on working:

> He makes grass grow for the cattle,
> and plants for people to cultivate –
> bringing forth food from the earth.
> (Psalm 104:14)

The Lord Jesus was on this earth for thirty-three years to do the work his Father had given him to do. I wonder how many of those years were spent in the carpenter's shop?

Followers of God are followers of a worker. Imitators of Christ are imitating a worker. This invests immense dignity in work. Adam and Eve, made in God's image, were immediately given physical work as their primary occupation in the Garden of Eden: 'The LORD God took the man and put him in the Garden of Eden to work it and take care of it' (Genesis 2:15). Work is not a result of sin, though we shall see in a moment that the Fall has had a huge impact on our work. Work was part of God's original design for us. One of the reasons why God created us was to be workers just like him.

People dream of making enough money to give up work, moving to a beautiful part of the world and putting their feet up for the rest of their days. 'Just imagine, no deadlines to enslave me. I will do what I like, when I like.' But inactivity satisfies no-one. The idea that eliminating work from our lives and increasing our leisure time as the key to freedom turns out to be a disappointing dream, an illusion. A change of pace from time to time can be refreshing, and a change of pace in retirement is often well deserved, but idleness, while attractive from a distance, will be found to be deeply frustrating. Not surprising really. God made us to be workers.

The cultural mandate

Humankind began work in a garden. But it was never God's intention for it to end there. A big God had a big plan in mind:

> So God created mankind in his own image,
>> in the image of God he created them;
>> male and female he created them.
>
> God blessed them and said to them, 'Be fruitful and increase in number; fill the earth and subdue it. Rule over the fish in the sea and the birds in the sky and over every living creature that moves on the ground.'
> (Genesis 1:27–28)

Adam and Eve were placed in the Garden of Eden to 'work it and take care of it' (Genesis 2:15). This applies not only to the land. God says, 'You are my image-bearers. Now fill the earth and subdue it. Go into the arts, sciences, literature, business and every aspect of the world. Be my image-bearers in marriage, family life and leisure activities. I want my world developed in such a way that my glory will be seen wherever people look.' Theologians like to call this our 'cultural mandate'. It's part of our mission as we live in this world.

A divine calling

Rather than a necessary evil, work is a divine calling. The whole of our life is to be dedicated to the glory of God.

What will it mean for us to work in this way? Well, it will certainly mean living distinctive, holy lives, and looking for opportunities to witness where we work. But it will mean so much more besides. When we do our work well, that in itself will glorify God and contribute to the world he has made. We will serve people through our work, making life more effective for them.

Greg Forster asks us to imagine someone working on a machine. His job is to pull a lever on that machine many times each day at the right time. 'The tendency is simply to think that pulling a lever means I will get paid. That's what work is all about, after all. But we must urge people to think, "What does this lever do?" If we don't, people will live in a very small world where they fail to see the reality of what's going on. Let's say that that lever makes a component for a car braking system. We want workers to be thinking, "OK, what I'm doing is making safer cars, and because cars are safer, the customers are willing to pay more for them, so that's why I get paid to do this. That's why they give me this money." But once we see the whole system, then we will understand that the bigger significance of what I'm doing is making the world a better place by making safer cars. The wages are a by-product of making cars safer.'[1]

The wages of course are not unimportant. Supporting your household is a very important biblical imperative (see 1 Timothy 5:8). When we support our households by doing good honest work, serve people and make the world a better place, we glorify God and get to the essence of the biblical purpose of work. As John Stott said, 'Every honourable work . . . needs to be seen by Christians as some kind of cooperation with God, in which we share with him in the transformation of the world, which he has made and committed to our care.'[2]

Work and the Fall

If work is so good, then why is it often so frustrating? We know that many find their work very stressful. Others find it very boring. Not all workers are angels, and not all bosses are archangels! Let's go back to Genesis again:

> To Adam he [God] said, 'Because you listened to your wife and ate from the tree about which I commanded you, "You must not eat from it,"

> 'Cursed is the ground because of you;
>   through painful toil you will eat food from it
>   all the days of your life.
> It will produce thorns and thistles for you,
>   and you will eat the plants of the field.
> By the sweat of your brow
>   you will eat your food
> until you return to the ground,
>   since from it you were taken;
> for dust you are
>   and to dust you will return.'
> (Genesis 3:17–19)

Work is not as God intended it to be. It has been damaged and degraded by the Fall. Thorns and thistles in the ground may be the equivalent of stress or boredom or an ungrateful boss or a lazy worker for us today. After the Fall, human work had the potential to produce materials and instruments which would cause destruction in God's world rather than 'take care of it'. Soon a city would be built, with the tower of Babel dominating it as an expression of human pride and in direct disobedience to God's will: 'Come, let us build ourselves a city, with a tower that reaches to the heavens, so that we may make a name for ourselves; otherwise we will be scattered over the face of the whole earth' (Genesis 11:4).

In our fallen world today, work is idolized. It is seen as the way of salvation on both a personal and societal level. Increased production will bring us the peace and freedom we are all searching for. This idolizing of work often leaves those who are not in paid employment feeling useless and without purpose and value. It can leave those whose primary work is in the home feeling like second-class citizens. So it is important to recognize that men and women were created in God's image before they were given work to do (Genesis 1:27–28). Human worth does not depend on work. And work is far more than paid employment. 'Taking care' of God's world gives 'work' a very broad definition. Those called to do this in the home are making a huge and an invaluable contribution. Those without paid employment can make an equally significant contribution.

'Taking care' of God's world gives 'work' a very broad definition.

I think of someone who lost her paid job and took some time out to find another. She spent that time between jobs working in a charity shop. She saw herself in that role as recycling goods, making a contribution to the alleviation of poverty in the world and being a blessing to others. She had such a positive approach to customers that many were encouraged through their contact with her.

So work is both good and bad. Like everything else in this fallen world, it's in need of being redeemed. Actually, it is being redeemed, and it will finally be redeemed one day.

Work redeemed

Work is being redeemed as God's people appreciate its place and purpose and begin to approach all their work for his glory.

We know it will be finally, fully redeemed. It's interesting that in that wonderful picture of the eternal city, the New Jerusalem, 'the kings of the earth will bring their splendour into it' (Revelation 21:24). Not all that we've been 'working and taking care of' will be lost. We may go on working and developing what we've been doing here for the glory of God, right into the new heaven and the new earth! It will be part of the redemption of creation:

> For the creation was subjected to frustration, not by its own choice, but by the will of the one who subjected it, in hope that the creation itself will be liberated from its bondage to decay and brought into the freedom and glory of the children of God.
> (Romans 8:20–21)

In eternity we will continue to fulfil the cultural mandate, though then without sin's destructive influence. Swords and spears will be made into ploughshares and pruning hooks (Micah 4:3). Can you begin to imagine the beautiful and beneficial things that will be made with the raw material of God's renewed creation?

When you look at work through this biblical lens, even the most mundane tasks can be filled with new meaning and significance. I sometimes wonder if one reason why many Christians get bored, and in their boredom look for satisfaction in things they will ultimately regret, is that they've never really understood the significant purpose God has for them in their place of work where they spend so much of their lives.

Questions

1. As you think about your abilities, experience and training up to this point, do you believe you are serving the Lord where he wants you?
2. 'Commissioned to go into your place of work.' Does that make you feel differently about your workplace?

Books

Darrell Cosden, *The Heavenly Good of Earthly Work* (Paternoster Press, 2006).

Mark Greene, *Thank God It's Monday: Ministry in the Workplace* (Scripture Union, 2010).

Timothy Keller, *Every Good Endeavour: Connecting Your Work to God's Plan for the World* (Hodder & Stoughton, 2012).

11

Spiritual disciplines

It wasn't how we had planned it, but the completion of our house sale came just before an intensely busy time in our lives. We had to move into our new home just a few days before leaving for three weeks at the Keswick Convention in the Lake District and then a five-week preaching tour of Australia, New Zealand and Canada. There was much to do, and looking back, Win and I had different goals. My attitude was: 'Let's just get in and leave our stuff. We can sort it all out when we get back.' Win wanted to do things in such a way that we wouldn't have to start from scratch when we got back. As usual, she was right, and it only took a little bit more thought and planning to do things the way she wanted, but my mind was on the Convention and my plans for the long journey. We were so busy, we hardly had time to talk, and that was the problem. With no communication, the relationship became strained, and tensions rose. Before it got too bad, we realized what was happening, stopped and had a heart-to-heart.

It takes time

We have seen that relationship is the essence of discipleship, and time is the key ingredient in maintaining and developing that relationship. When looking at the subject of time, we noticed that it seems that there is a lot less of it around these days. Nonsense, of course, as there are still twenty-four hours in each day, but so many more things are pressing in on that time, all competing for a slice of it. The greatest challenge in my years of walking with Jesus has been making those decisions that will give me focused time in his presence. I have found that although I know I live every moment in his presence, I need to pause regularly throughout the day to remind myself of this reality.

The gym I used to attend included a steam room. But my routine did not allow for such luxuries. I found that I could have a really good workout, eat a sandwich and be back at my desk in seventy minutes. As I passed the guys relaxing in the steam room, I wondered if they had any purpose in life at all! Later a regular pause in the presence of God became important to me, and the gym visits lasted ninety minutes, with ten in the steam room, relaxing in a focused way in the presence of God. Today I consider focused times in the presence of Jesus as one of the great privileges of life: the coffee break, the bike ride, the brief walk, the first and last moments of the day. I have a friend who uses the hour alarm on his wristwatch as a reminder just to pause and recognize the presence of Jesus. Without such times of intentional stopping, I find it's not long before I am doing my own thing, living for self, not for Jesus.

Win and I enjoy few things more than the coffee shop. We love coffee, but an extended time to be together and talk is even more special. I need the same in my walk with Jesus. Not necessarily coffee, but certainly extended time.

The quiet time

I have sought, with varying degrees of success, to maintain a daily extended time with the Lord. Christians have traditionally called this 'the quiet time'. I am a morning person. I love to be up early and on a particular seat in my study to start the day with Jesus. There have been times when this might have been the dream but not the reality. I have already mentioned my time as a young dad. There were only ten and a half months between our first two children. (That was before we balanced our view of the sovereignty of God with human responsibility!) First thing in the morning our beautiful babies quite rightly demanded our attention. Isn't it great to know that the Lord understands these different seasons of our lives and the varying demands upon us? In those days when we had three small children, I had a demanding job, and the house we had bought needed a great deal of work just to make it habitable. We had no washing machine in the early years, though we had plenty of nappies! Survival was success. If we could get some quiet focused time with the Lord, we grabbed it, but often it just didn't happen. What's the difference between legalism and discipline? That question might take some time to answer, but I know that if I had insisted on an early-morning quiet time during those days and been racked with guilt if it didn't happen, I would have been suffering from legalism. If you are not a morning person, that's fine. Be who you are! Maybe lunchtime or evening will work best for your quiet time. Whatever works for you, do it, but make sure you do find something that works for you.

Practical tips

Certain things are really helpful in maintaining this discipline. I mentioned a particular chair in my study. It is good to find not only the best time for you, but also the best place. Look for somewhere comfortable where you have the best opportunity of being undisturbed. If you are like me, then distractions will be a big issue. No sooner have you settled down than things you need to do in that day, or forgot to do the previous day, flood into your mind. Keep a notebook in which to write those things down, for action later. I love as much variety as possible. Use recorded worship songs, and don't be afraid to sing along with them, although if you are a morning person and the rest of the family are not, have a little mercy! I have periods when I use liturgy. Sometimes I read a large portion of Scripture; at other times I meditate on one verse. I think that learning the art of meditation is a great help. Meditating on Scripture means looking at the verse or phrase from every angle, asking questions about it: what does this tell me about God, myself, the world I am living in? If I truly believe what I am reading here, what do I need to do? A great help in meditating is to memorize the verse itself. At other times I work through a book as well as reading Scripture. Sometimes I just read from a particular point in the Bible, asking the Lord to emphasize one verse or even one phrase as I read, and then I stop and meditate on it. A biography can be an inspiration and give a worked-out example of someone walking with God. Some like a structure for these times. One simple model is to start with adoration, then move to confession, then thanksgiving and finally supplication.

Can I get a word in?

Remember, this is a relationship. But it's not much of a relationship if one person is doing all the talking! Learn the art of listening. I often have to slow down consciously and clear my mind of a number of things if I am going to be able to listen properly. Breathing exercises can be helpful: something as simple as inhaling as much as you can and slowly exhaling for a few moments. Remember your notebook for writing down things that are in your mind, in the hope that once you've written them down, they will no longer dominate your thinking.

You need to get out more

Now my chair in the study is great, but there is also God's big and beautiful creation out there. A quiet time in a beautiful place can be truly special:

> The heavens declare the glory of God;
> the skies proclaim the work of his hands.
> Day after day they pour forth speech;
> night after night they reveal knowledge.
> (Psalm 19:1–2)

To get out of the study, living room, bedroom or whatever, and enjoy creation, watching and listening to the Lord declaring his glory there, can be an unforgettable experience.

Worship: what we were made for

Worship will result as we respond to God revealing himself through his Word and his world. This is what we were created for. This is what God longs to receive from us. Jesus told the woman he met at the well in Sychar that the Father was seeking for worshippers (John 4:23). Don't you want to be one of those whom the Father is seeking? There is no greater pleasure for us as parents than spending time with our children. Isn't it almost beyond belief that we can bring something to our Father? We can bring him pleasure:

Ascribe to the LORD the glory due to his name;
  bring an offering and come before him.
Worship the LORD in the splendour of his holiness.
(1 Chronicles 16:29)

Healthy choices

What the Lord wants from us is also the best thing for us. Time with the Lord is crucial to our spiritual health.

I believe many of you reading this know it is true, yet you still struggle to make time. Satan is committed to keep you involved in a multitude of other things. A preacher once asked thousands of Christian leaders, 'What normally emerges in the life of a person who neglects his or her spiritual life?' The answers that came back were not surprising: tiredness, joylessness and impatience. It was a pretty depressing list. She wrote them down on the whiteboard to her left. Then another question: 'What emerges in your life when you are deeply connected with God?' Again, no surprises as she wrote the answers on the board to her right: it was the opposite of what she had just written. Then, pointing to the list on the left, she asked who voted for the life with these results. No hands were raised. She continued, 'We all make choices every day, leading to one of the two results we see here. Though none of you has voted for the life that results in tiredness and joylessness, in reality many of you are daily making the choices which lead exactly to those results.'

One of my deep desires in writing this book is that you might take out your daily schedule and write your quiet time into it. Make this a daily appointment. It's the health decision that will bring joy to God. A regular spiritual retreat will also be hugely beneficial. It might start with just a few hours, but often it will progress from there. I have sought over the years to spend a half-day in a beautiful place and, less regularly, a full day. I spend this time in worship, reflection, reading and seeking to listen to God. I have friends who have benefitted from one-week retreats. These have normally taken place in some retreat centre or other and have had at least a degree of direction from someone with experience in that area.

Breakfast or big fast?

One of our children didn't walk with Jesus at one stage. Another has had a long struggle with health issues. When I led a large mission organization like OM, there were invariably times of crisis among its members.

Fasting has been an important discipline for me at such times. My normal routine is to miss breakfast. This gives me longer to pray through the issue, and expresses to God just how important it is to me, and how I want to depend entirely on him as I seek the answer. Fasting has many other benefits too. It is a way of stating our authority over our bodily desires. Why do

Our bodily desires are mastering us.

we fail in the areas of too much screen time, pornography, greed, and so much more? Our bodily desires are mastering us. The spiritual discipline of fasting teaches us that we can master those desires not just by repressing them, but by rechannelling them into something so much more wonderful and ultimately completely satisfying.

Like every spiritual discipline, however, fasting can become a hindrance rather than a help. The moment you begin to take pride in your fasting, it becomes a hindrance to your walk with God. Remember,

When you fast, do not look sombre as the hypocrites do, for they disfigure their faces to show others they are fasting. Truly I tell you, they have received their reward in full. But when you fast, put oil on your head and wash your face, so that it will not be obvious to others that you are fasting, but only to your Father, who is unseen; and your Father, who sees what is done in secret, will reward you.

(Matthew 6:16–18)

We have recognized a number of spiritual disciplines: prayer, study, solitude, worship, fasting, but there are also many more that might encourage you in your walk with God. (See, for example, the books mentioned at the end of this chapter for a much wider and fuller introduction to the spiritual disciplines.) These disciplines have no merit in themselves, but they do have a great purpose: to encourage us into the presence of our wonderful, amazing God.

Questions

1. What steps can you take to build into your life regular focused, uncluttered time with God, if this is not already your regular practice?
2. What is normally called the 'Lord's Prayer' might be better called the 'pattern prayer'. Study this pattern and see what you can learn for your own prayer life (Matthew 6:9–13).

Books

Richard Foster, *Life with God* (Hodder & Stoughton, 2009).
Dallas Willard, *Renovation of the Heart: Putting on the Character of Christ* (IVP, 2002).

12

Community

As in the time of the judges in Israel, so it is in the church today. Each person does what is good in his or her own eyes. If Christians today could recover even half of the profound New Testament understanding of the church as community, we would discover a powerful protection against the pervasive individualism that devastates the Western church . . . God's grand strategy of redemption does not focus on redeeming isolated individuals; it centres on the creation of a new people, a new community, a new social order that begins to live now the way the Creator intended.[1]

I was born and brought up in the Western world, in a culture where individualism reigns. Now I'm not just Western, but English, and worldwide it is known that the Englishman's home is his castle. We are never more comfortable than when we can enter our 'castles', pull up the drawbridge and continue with our private lives.

I was brought up to believe that my relationship with God was all that I needed to focus on in order to live the Christian life. I was inspired by stories of Christians who had been kept in solitary confinement for years, sustained only by the presence of God. All they had was God, and that was enough!

But if God was sufficient, then what was the place of my brothers and sisters in my Christian growth? The idea that God might meet some of my needs through them, or that they had a contribution to make to my spiritual growth, was not strongly emphasized.

Indeed, I grew up thinking that admitting needs and problems in my Christian life was a sign of spiritual weakness. For anyone to acknowledge, for example, that they were struggling with a period of depression seemed to be the very antithesis of being evangelical. After all, had we not been saved from a life of struggle to experience the joy and freedom of Christ? More than once I heard the whisper that such depression could only have a demonic cause. Testimony meetings were popular in those days, and they left me believing that the Christian life should be plain sailing, and if you were struggling, there were serious things that needed to be addressed. The words 'wonderful' and 'marvellous' punctuated those testimonies. All this added to my problems, because my Christian life as a teenager was far from wonderful. I never struggled with depression admittedly, but there were questions and issues in my life about which I felt I had better keep my mouth shut.

One anothering

It's amazing how far we can stray from what the Christian life was intended to be. No-one reading the Bible for the first time would ever think that it was to be lived in a vacuum. Christianity is all about a relationship with God, but it's also about a relationship with the people of God. In Ephesians 2:13–14 we see that our being reconciled to God through Christ should also lead to reconciliation in our human relationships: 'But now in Christ Jesus you who once were far away have been brought near by the blood of Christ. For he himself is our peace, who has made the two groups one and has destroyed the barrier, the dividing wall of hostility.' Jew and Gentile, separated by a huge cultural chasm, were united in Christ. The unified body of believers was intended to be a powerful witness to the gospel and a place of encouragement and growth. God, who himself lives in the perfect community of the Trinity (three persons: Father, Son and Holy Spirit), never planned to redeem isolated individuals. As we will see in the next chapter, when we look at mission, God's plan has always been to redeem a people whose lives *together* would glorify him in the world. The Trinity is a perfect model for this community, and we are called to mirror the perfect unity that we see there.

As you know, travel has been for me an ever-present reality for decades. If you are involved in leading a mission, working in more than a hundred countries, this goes with the job. Through all those years I did my very best to be committed to a local church. I hope I made some contribution to that church, but there is no doubt whatsoever in my mind that the influence of the church on me was huge. It was particularly important for me to have this commitment. One of the dangers of constant travel and being in the public limelight is that you spend a lot of time with people who don't know you. You come to them as a leader and a preacher, and the tendency is for them to place you on some kind of pedestal. I would often be speaking on mission and church issues. How should mission be accomplished? How can the church play its full part in the mission of God? Again, the great danger is that we are constantly talking to others about these matters, but never actually doing them ourselves.

My involvement too in a local church back home with people who knew me and had known me for years was vital for keeping my feet on the ground, and this place was crucial for my growth as a disciple. In my home church there was no pedestal for me, because I was treated as an equal.

But local church life was not easy. Growing together with people of different personalities, from different backgrounds, sometimes with different theological convictions, can be 'interesting' to say the least. Sometimes it can be so difficult that it is easy to walk away from it. In fact, that seems to be a trend today, and as we saw earlier, we live in a society where commitment is only to the degree that it suits *me*. But disciples of Jesus must be committed to the people of Jesus. We are called to be part of the body of Christ, so commitment to the members of that body should go without saying. We see from the earliest days of the church that commitment to Christ meant commitment to the community of Christ: 'The Lord added to their number daily those who were being saved' (Acts 2:47), and they were a committed community – committed to one another (verses 45–46), and committed to their Lord (verses 46–47).

John Wesley, the founder of Methodism, insisted that new converts join small groups or classes. They met weekly and held one another accountable as they encouraged each other in their spiritual growth. It was Wesley's view that the level of commitment to that group was a sign of how genuine the conversion had been. For almost 150 years Methodists were among the fastest-growing groups of Christians in the world – the power of being together in Christ in community was clearly evident.

I believe that if you are serious in your desire to be a disciple of Christ, then evidence of that will be seen in your commitment to a local expression of his body: a local church.

Commitment will mean more than attendance, more than membership. You will be concerned to see the growth of the body, and that means encouraging, caring for and being willing to challenge one another, with spiritual development as the goal:

> Let us consider how we may spur one another on towards love and good deeds, not giving up meeting together, as some are in the habit of doing, but encouraging one another – and all the more as you see the Day approaching.
> (Hebrews 10:24–25)

Earlier, we looked at the gifts of the Holy Spirit. We saw that every Christian has been given these. The context in which they are given is the body of Christ. And they are gifts for the body, given to build up the body. Growth in the body will be the inevitable result if each member of the body uses his or her gifts for the good of the body: 'From him the whole body, joined and held together by every supporting ligament, grows and builds itself up in love, as each part does its work' (Ephesians 4:16). But is it not the case in many churches that if you took away a handful of people, the church would cease to function? Many are passengers, not involved; gifts lie dormant, and the church and the world suffer because of it.

Focus: the early caring, sharing church

In this Western culture, not only does individualism reign, but it is praised too. Self-made men and women are admired. There is little time or place for deep, vulnerable friendships. Such friendships can even be seen as a bit strange and questionable, especially if they are of the same-gender variety. Sin isolates us. It separates us from God, from true relationship with one another, and even from a true understanding and acceptance of ourselves. Redemption, on the other hand, is all about relationship: restored relationship with God, authentic, committed relationship within the body, and self-acceptance as redeemed children of God.

There is no question that Jesus and his apostles saw community as the context for making disciples. Jesus himself created a close-knit community. His disciples travelled together, and lived and failed together. They all lived out of a common financial fund. It was within the context of this community that the faith of the disciples grew.

A remarkable feature of the early chapters of the Acts of the Apostles is the deeply shared life of the early Christians:

> They devoted themselves to the apostles' teaching and to fellowship, to the breaking of bread and to prayer. Everyone was filled with awe at the many wonders and signs performed by the apostles. All the believers were together and had everything in common. They sold property and possessions to give to anyone who had need. Every day they continued to meet together in the temple courts. They broke bread in their homes and ate together with glad and sincere hearts, praising God and enjoying the favour of all the people. And the Lord added to their number daily those who were being saved.
> (Acts 2:42–47)

This was a unique time in the development of the Christian church, and not all the aspects of this deeply shared life are intended to be replicated in every era. But the aspects of Christian community seen here in Acts 2 are essential to every believer who wants to grow in Christ. Those early disciples were a learning community. They desired to have time together to worship, pray and spend time in the Word. They ate together and shared in Holy Communion together. There was a desire to minister to each other's practical needs. They had developed a caring, sharing community. You can imagine that this was a safe place where they could share honestly and openly. And the community was clearly a very joyful place too.

We need community because there is so much we can learn from one another. This is the place where character is shaped and developed. And the hard times in community will often be as important as the good ones.

The tendency in the church in many parts of the world is for Christians to come together once a week. There is a time of 'worship': mainly singing, some teaching and then a handshake or even an embrace as you leave, and that's it. A church leader recently said, 'Our church is wide, broad and diverse, but I couldn't say it's deep.' Could that be said of your church?

Growth groups

A number of years ago my family helped me to realize that my life was out of balance. I was busy, so much so that some of the essentials were being neglected. Family life was one of those essentials, but so too was the developing of true friend-ships. I had hundreds of acquaintances, but few of what I would now call fruitful friendships.

It is difficult, if not impossible, to get to know more than eight or ten people in depth at any one time. That's why small groups in churches are vital. If you are serious about disciple-ship, then you need to ask, 'Do I have a group of friends with whom I can share my life, my joys, problems, questions, doubts, fears, victories and failures, a group in which I would be able to share such things, knowing these people would pray for me and offer any advice they had to give? And will they speak the 'truth in love' when I need it (Ephesians 4:15)?

Friends like this look out for you. They care enough to question and challenge you when necessary. They are indeed prepared to 'speak the truth in love'. Being an introvert, I still struggle to develop such friendships, and I know I'm not alone. Surveys have shown that though this is by no means exclusively a male problem, women tend to be much better at sharing their lives than men. The few friendships that men do develop revolve around doing things together, preferably fast, all-consuming things, delivering us possibly from the very priority we are talking about: truly sharing our lives.

I sat down with a friend a few days ago, and we discussed the areas of temptation in our lives that we felt Satan would concentrate on as he sought to bring us down. We had to be very honest and open with each other, but the bigger intention was spiritual development for each other.

A couple of years ago I was travelling in Asia with a fellow Christian whom I knew and trusted. There I spoke at a conference alongside another speaker. After the meeting I spoke to my colleague, and we agreed that the other speaker had really missed the mark in his message. (We didn't talk about my message of course!) Later in the evening we had a meal with the other speaker, and I complimented him on his message. My very good friend challenged me later about my integrity, and asked whether I felt I was really helping this brother by my remarks.

A committed, open, honest community is the context for strong discipleship growth. It's also an amazing witness in a world that is crying out for relationship and community.

The church as a body in the New Testament is such an important illustration. We saw earlier how each part needs the rest of the body for healthy development: I need the body in order to grow, and the rest of the body needs me. If, however, I choose to stay in my castle with the drawbridge raised, not only am I losing out, but others are missing out as well.

Within the safety of a committed community, we can 'speak the truth in love to one another'. When my family spoke to me about my life being out of kilter, that is what they were doing. I knew they loved me and wanted the best for me. In that safe context, their words were transforming.

As Jonathan Lamb says,

> One of the characteristics of genuine Christian fellowship in our churches or organizations will be open hearts. We can usually tell that this is a feature of healthy community by such practical signs as open homes, not formal relationships; open fellowship, not special in-groups; open communication which confronts as well as encourages, not innuendo and gossip . . . Opening our hearts wide is an essential part of Christian integrity and represents an attractive feature of Christian community which commends the gospel in an age of fractured relationships.[2]

Do you have relationships that encourage your spiritual growth? If not, begin to pray that God will lead you to those with whom you could form such a group. If your church has small groups, then join one. This might be God's group for your spiritual development and in which you can make a contribution to the development of others.

Questions

1. What can we learn for our relationships with one another from the model of the relationship within the Trinity?

2. Are we ready to be truly honest with others about ourselves? If not, could this be a sign that we are not certain that God accepts us as we are?

Books

Sam Allberry, *Connected: Living in the Light of the Trinity* (IVP, 2012).

John Stott, *The Living Church: Convictions of a Lifelong Pastor* (Leicester: IVP, 2007).

13

Mission

Bill Watterson, author of the comic strip *Calvin and Hobbs*, was asked whether he thought there was a God. He replied, 'Well, someone's out to get me!'[1]

Outrageous grace

God is not out to get us but to bless us, and what is more, he is committed to blessing the whole world. This is a long-standing commitment. Thousands of years ago he said to a no doubt highly surprised Abraham, 'I'm going to bless you, and through you the whole world' (see Genesis 12:3).

To see where that promise appears in history is to recognize the outrageous grace of God. The first eleven chapters of Genesis are a disaster account. After the Fall and the flood, humankind is rebelling once again. God had said to Noah after the flood, 'Be fruitful and increase in number; multiply on the earth and increase upon it' (Genesis 9:7). Initially, things went well. From the clans of Noah, nations were spreading out over the earth (Genesis 10:32). But as we have seen, humankind soon slipped back into their old ways: 'Come, let us build ourselves a city, with a tower that reaches to the heavens, so that we may make a name for ourselves; otherwise we will be scattered over the face of the whole earth' (Genesis 11:4).

Imagine you were reading the Bible for the first time and you were turning the page from Genesis 11 to Genesis 12. What might you be expecting? An account of God washing his hands of the whole humanity project? 'I've had enough of their constant rebellion.' But instead of an account of destruction, you have the promise of global blessing which no people on earth will miss. This is the God we worship and serve, and this is why the mission of God to redeem a fallen creation is at the heart of the Bible story.

It's interesting to see who God chooses to use as his instruments for this global blessing: an elderly childless couple. From them, according to the promise, there will come a nation which God will use to bless all nations. He uses the most surprising people. He loves to use 'the weak things of the world to shame the strong' (1 Corinthians 1:27).

The plan

But how will God redeem this fallen creation? In Genesis 18:18 God repeats his promise that Abraham will become a powerful nation and all nations will be blessed through him. Then in verse 19 he explains how: 'For I have chosen him, so that he will direct his children and his household after him to keep the way of the LORD by doing what is right and just, so that the LORD will bring about for Abraham what he has promised him.' The household of Abraham was to be a small model community living in obedience to the ways of God in the middle of a fallen creation.

That family would develop into a nation. God wanted a model nation living in obedience to his ways, and by their difference from all the nations around them, they would become 'a light to the nations': 'If you obey me fully and keep my covenant, then out of all nations you will be my treasured possession. Although the whole earth is mine, you will be for me a kingdom of priests and a holy nation' (Exodus 19:5–6).

He wants Israel to be two things: priestly and holy. Priests in Israel stood in the middle, between God and the people. They were appointed to teach the ways of God, and to bless the people in the name of the Lord. Israel's calling to be a priestly people meant that God wanted to use them to bring his blessing and knowledge of him to the nations, and they would do this by being a holy nation. The word 'holy' means 'different', 'utterly distinct'. 'The LORD said to Moses, "Speak to the entire assembly of Israel and say to them: 'Be holy because I, the LORD your God, am holy'"' (Leviticus 19:1–2). The rest of the chapter shows how this was intended to impact upon every aspect of their lives, personally and as a community. It was, and is, fundamental to the mission of God that God has a people living in the world, shining like stars in the darkness.

Israel says 'No'

Tragically, Israel refused this divine calling. There was always a faithful remnant, but as a nation, they refused the calling to be different. We see an example of this in 1 Samuel 8:

> So all the elders of Israel gathered together and came to Samuel at Ramah. They said to him, 'You are old, and your sons do not follow your ways; now appoint a king to lead us, such as all the other nations have.'
>
> But when they said, 'Give us a king to lead us,' this displeased Samuel; so he prayed to the LORD. And the LORD

told him, 'Listen to all that the people are saying to you;
it is not you they have rejected, but they have rejected me
as their king.'

. . . But the people refused to listen to Samuel. 'No!' they
said. 'We want a king over us. Then we shall be like all the
other nations.'

(1 Samuel 8:4–7, 19)

Rather than being distinct among the nations, 'they rejected
his decrees and the covenants he had made with their ancestors
and the statutes he had warned them to keep . . . They imitated the nations around them' (2 Kings 17:15).

Mission and holiness can never be divorced.

Israel could not further the mission of God in his world without living as the people of God among the nations. Mission and holiness can never be divorced.

God's perfect servant

Is this the end of the road? Will God now give up on humanity?
Thankfully, no.

Here is my servant, whom, I uphold,
    my chosen one in whom I delight;
I will put my Spirit on him,
    and he will bring justice to the nations . . .
    he will not falter or be discouraged
till he establishes justice on the earth.
    In his teaching the islands will put their hope.
(Isaiah 42:1, 4)

God's purpose is not thwarted by the disobedience in Israel. The seed of Abraham, the Lord Jesus Christ, will live that utterly distinctive life and then become 'a curse for us . . . in order that the blessing given to Abraham might come to the Gentiles' (Galatians 3:13–14).

The light of God shines in the world through the utterly distinctive life of Jesus. But there is a problem. Fallen humanity hates the light: 'Light has come into the world, but people loved darkness instead of light because their deeds were evil. Everyone who does evil hates the light, and will not come into the light for fear that their deeds will be exposed' (John 3:19–20). The light of the world is nailed to a cross, but death cannot hold him. He rises from the dead, never to die again.

Eating with his disciples after his resurrection, he commands them, 'Do not leave Jerusalem, but wait for the gift my Father promised, which you have heard me speak about. For John baptised with water, but in a few days you will be baptised with the Holy Spirit' (Acts 1:4–5). We receive his Spirit so that we can be that light in the world today. 'You will receive power when the Holy Spirit comes on you; and you will be my witnesses in Jerusalem, and in all Judea and Samaria, and to the ends of the earth,' we read in verse 8.

The 'come' of mission

We cannot fulfil the mission of God without being his disciples. And if we are his disciples, then we must be involved in his mission. Is the tragedy today that we are in danger of repeating Israel's failure? Are we prepared to be that distinctive holy people in a fallen world? Now, it's not easy. Increasingly, it calls for a totally counter-cultural lifestyle. Most of us don't like to be different. It is so much easier just to blend in, so the danger of compromise is ever-present. It is right to emphasize the 'go' of mission, but there must also be the 'come' of mission. A people so enjoying God and one another in the family of God that the lifestyle is so distinctive and attractive, and the worship so authentic, that it becomes like a magnet, drawing people who want to be part of the action.

When Israel had been exiled from their land because of their refusal to be a holy people, the Word of the Lord came to them through the prophet Zechariah. First, he paints a picture of the people back in their land: 'This is what the LORD Almighty says: "Once again men and women of ripe old age will sit in the streets of Jerusalem, each of them with cane in hand because of their age. The city streets will be filled with boys and girls playing there"' (Zechariah 8:4–5). God is saying, if you will return to me, I will bring you back to the land. But that will just be the beginning:

> This is what the LORD Almighty says: 'Many peoples and the inhabitants of many cities will yet come, and the inhabitants of one city will go to another and say, "Let us go at once to entreat the LORD and seek the LORD Almighty. I myself am going." And many peoples and powerful nations will come to Jerusalem to seek the LORD Almighty and to entreat him.'
>
> This is what the LORD Almighty says: 'In those days ten people from all languages and nations will take firm hold of one Jew by the hem of his robe and say, "Let us go with you, because we have heard that God is with you."'
> (Zechariah 8:20–23)

This is God's strategy: a priestly, holy people showing forth his greatness and glory as they live distinctive, attractive lives together. God wants his witness throughout the whole world. That means in every nation and the whole of society.

This witness must be through both the life and the Word. There are some strange ideas being bandied about these days suggesting that proclaiming the gospel is somehow secondary to living it out.[2] We are encouraged to proclaim the gospel and, if necessary, use words! But lip and life must not be separated. We saw earlier the transforming power of the Word of God. Yes, we must live the life, demonstrating the message we proclaim, but we are called also to proclaim that message. It is a glorious message, not something we must use only if necessary. And every disciple will be a witness. We may not all have the gift of the evangelist, but surely Peter was right when he said to the Sanhedrin, 'We cannot help speaking about what we have seen and heard' (Acts 4:20). To be silent about something which we know to be life-changing now and eternally is to be unfaithful to God and to our fellow men and women.

The scope of mission

God's mission is not only to redeem people, but to redeem creation: a redeemed people living in a new heaven and a renewed earth is the goal. A biblical understanding of mission can be wrecked by the fatal secular-spiritual divide mentioned in chapter 6. This so easily leads to a view that God's mission is to be carried out by missionaries, individuals who manage to raise enough financial support from other Christians to leave their jobs and work full-time overseas. Their job is to evangelize: to bring the good news of Jesus to the people and build his church. Yet we fail to consider Christians engaged in the world of education, industry, commerce or bringing up children to be involved in the mission of God.

Do Christians have any other responsibility than to evangelize? What did God mean when he said he was going to bless the nations? Was that just the blessing of salvation? When God speaks about his people 'seeking the welfare of the city' (see Jeremiah 29:7) when they were in exile, what exactly did he mean? When he called us to be salt and light in society, what exactly does that involve?

The problem with the dichotomy in the minds of many Christians is that it leaves them thinking that they are spending most of their time doing things that have nothing to do with the mission of God.

Think of Daniel, carried off into exile in Babylon. He attains a privileged position in the royal palace. He could have spent all his time wondering why he was there and what possible good he could do in such a foreign and wicked culture, but he didn't. Was he influenced by a letter sent from the prophet Jeremiah not too long after the first wave of exiles was taken to Babylon?

> This is what the LORD Almighty, the God of Israel, says to all those I carried into exile from Jerusalem to Babylon: 'Build houses and settle down; plant gardens and eat what they produce. Marry and have sons and daughters; find wives for your sons and give your daughters in marriage, so that they too may have sons and daughters. Increase in number there; do not decrease. Also, seek the peace and prosperity of the city to which I have carried you into exile. Pray to the LORD for it, because if it prospers, you too will prosper.'
> (Jeremiah 29:4–7)

Daniel certainly worked for the welfare of the people he lived amongst. Successive kings recognized his God-given gifts and elevated him to positions where he would have a massive impact on Babylonian society. Consider this simple statement which greatly influenced me some years ago: 'Wherever the people of the kingdom are active, some people will be converted, but everyone will be blessed.'

Does this give a new understanding to the mission of God and your role in it? It's not just something for paid missionaries. God has promised to bless, and he wants you to bring his blessing into every situation where he sends you. He wants every church to be a source of blessing in the community where it is placed.

The 'go' of mission

The global nature of both the promise of God and the commission of Christ cannot, however, be ignored: 'All nations of people will be blessed. Start in Jerusalem, but don't stop until the ends of the earth are reached' (see Acts 1:8). The wonderful news for us as followers of Jesus is that thousands are joining us every day. As already noted, these are incredible days of harvest in the kingdom of God. What were referred to as 'the mission fields' in my youth now house the fastest-growing churches in the world, and they are now sending out missionaries by the thousands.

But with all this growth, thousands of people groups still have no indigenous group of believers worshipping God. That is why pioneer missions are still a great priority. John Piper writes, 'Mission exists because worship doesn't.'[3] This is the primary motive for mission. Obedience to the Great Commission is a valid motive, as is the concern for the lostness of humanity, but zeal for the glory of Christ must always be our primary motivation. Wherever he is not receiving the worship he alone deserves, mission is required. That means that people groups where there are no true worshippers, and any areas of our society where Jesus is receiving no honour, must take priority. Not only is this for the glory of God, it is also for his gladness. As J. I. Packer says,

> God was happy without men, before man was made. He would have continued happy, had he simply destroyed men after men had sinned, but as it is, he set his love upon particular sinners and this means that by his own voluntary choice he will not know perfect and unmixed happiness again until he has brought every one of them to heaven. He has, in effect, resolved that henceforth through all eternity his happiness shall be conditional upon ours.[4]

The cost of mission

I believe that our response to the call to mission will be one of the great tests of our discipleship. It is increasingly uncomfortable to state in public: 'For all people there is only one Saviour.' The peoples of the world must be encouraged to 'follow their own way'. It is considered arrogant and intolerant to suggest that they must leave their chosen way and follow the One who declared, 'I am the way and the truth and the life' (John 14:6). It seems that in our culture, which prides itself in its tolerance, the only thing we cannot tolerate is the truth of the uniqueness of Christ. Christ's disciples will have to make their decision: are we going to bow to the spirit of the age, or before the commands of our King? The message of Christ's uniqueness and the need to proclaim it cannot be denied by anyone who takes the Word of God seriously.

Peter, filled with the Holy Spirit, speaks to the Sanhedrin who want to silence him. But Peter would not be silent. Why? 'Salvation is found in no one else, for there is no other name under heaven given to mankind by which we must be saved' (Acts 4:12).

As Jesus called his first disciples, the mission he was calling them to was clear: 'Come, follow me . . . and I will send you out to fish for people' (Matthew 4:19). As he prepared to leave his disciples, there was no change in that calling. All four of the Gospel writers agree that the final words of Jesus to his followers expressed his concern that the good news be taken to the ends of the earth (Matthew 28:19; Mark 16:15; Luke 24:47; John 20:21).

I often wonder if the reason why many Christians do not find life fulfilling, the reason why we get involved in watching things we shouldn't be watching, listening to things we should never be listening to, engaging in activities that destroy our Christian testimony, is that we have never found our place in the mission of God. We are therefore not fulfilling the purpose for which we exist. Frankly, I cannot understand how any Christian who understands the mission of God can ever be bored!

Discipleship which does not result in mission is not true discipleship at all. And true mission can only be engaged in by those committed to true discipleship.

It seems fitting to quote from John Stott, that global missionary statesman to whom we owe so much, when concluding our study of mission in the context of discipleship:

There are the five parts of the Bible. The God of the Old Testament is a missionary God, calling one family in order to bless all the families of the earth. The Christ of the Gospels is a missionary Christ; he sent the church out to witness. The Spirit of the Acts is a missionary Spirit; he drove the church out from Jerusalem to Rome. The church of the Epistles is a missionary church, a worldwide community with a worldwide vocation. The end of the Revelation is a missionary end, a countless throng from every nation. So I think we have to say the religion of the Bible is a missionary religion. The evidence is overwhelming and irrefutable. Mission cannot be regarded as a regrettable lapse from tolerance or decency. Mission cannot be regarded as the hobby of a few fanatical eccentrics in the church. Mission lies at the heart of God and therefore at the very heart of the church. A church without mission is no longer a church. It is contradicting an essential part of its identity. The church *is* mission.[5]

Questions

1. Write down in one paragraph what you believe to be the mission of God in the world. Then spend time considering how you are involved in that mission.
2. The need to send missionaries to those peoples who have no indigenous church is urgent. But where in the world are those people groups? Do some research on these groups. Look at *Operation World* and websites such as Joshuaproject.net.

Books

Jason Mandryk, *Operation World: The Definitive Prayer Guide to Every Nation*, 7th edn (IVP USA, 2012).
Christopher J. H. Wright, *The Mission of God's People: A Biblical Theology of the Church's Mission* (Zondervan, 2010).

A final word
Jesus: the reason

Thank you for travelling with me through this brief book. My motive in writing it was to stimulate both writer and readers to keep going deeper and further in our journey with Jesus.

Some books that I have read on the subject have left me feeling exhausted: the challenge and cost of discipleship have seemed so enormous. Yet I trust I have not underplayed that element in any way.

The call that demands everything of us is in fact the call to deep rest.

I do believe Bonhoeffer was right: 'When Christ calls a man, he bids him come and die.'[1] But I sincerely hope that, along with the challenge, I have shown that this call to 'come and die' is actually the call to life. The call that demands everything of us is in fact the call to deep rest. The call to die to sin is the call to life with God, resting in the finished work of Christ and an utterly secure future.

The two statements of Jesus that follow may seem on first reading to be in opposition to each other, but I trust you now see them as perfectly complementary:

Then Jesus said to his disciples, 'Whoever wants to be my disciple must deny themselves and take up their cross and follow me.'
(Matthew 16:24)

Come to me, all you who are weary and burdened, and I will give you rest. Take my yoke upon you and learn from me, for I am gentle and humble in heart, and you will find rest for your souls. For my yoke is easy and my burden is light.
(Matthew 11:28–30)

I hope you have been excited by the 'resources' mentioned. Jesus himself leads us on the journey through his Spirit within us. As we walk through life 'in step with the Spirit', the Word of God is always there, and these are our two constant companions.

I hope that the emphasis on discipleship as a relationship has been clear. Discipleship programmes are great, and I love structure and programmes myself. But if fulfilling the programme becomes a goal in itself, then we've failed. The goal is to know Jesus better, an ever-deeper and more authentic relationship.

I've been under a tight deadline to get this manuscript finished. This morning in my quiet time, realizing I probably could finish today and feeling a bit weary, I put my Bible reading plan to one side, and sitting on my usual study chair, I spent half an hour relaxing and consciously focusing my thoughts on Jesus himself, his majesty and power and the awesome privilege of BEING WITH HIM.

Eventually, I turned to Revelation 1 and the amazing description of his majesty:

> I turned round to see the voice that was speaking to me. And when I turned I saw seven golden lampstands, and among the lampstands was someone like a son of man, dressed in a robe reaching down to his feet and with a golden sash round his chest. The hair on his head was white like wool, as white as snow, and his eyes were like blazing fire. His feet were like bronze glowing in a furnace, and his voice was like the sound of rushing waters. In his right hand he held seven stars, and coming out of his mouth was a sharp, double-edged sword. His face was like the sun shining in all its brilliance.
> (Revelation 1:12–16)

Jesus was right there in the middle of the life of those churches mentioned in verse 11. Most of them were facing hard times, but he was right there with them.

That's the sheer privilege of discipleship, and that's why DISCIPLESHIP MATTERS. It's all about being with him.

He will be with us all throughout the journey until he takes us home.

Notes

Introduction: Cheap grace

1. Ronald J. Sider, *The Scandal of the Evangelical Conscience: Why Are Christians Living Just Like the Rest of the World?* (Baker, 2005).
2. Dietrich Bonhoeffer, *The Cost of Discipleship* (SCM, 2001).

1. Born again

1. Ronald J. Sider, *The Scandal of the Evangelical Conscience: Why Are Christians Living Just Like the Rest of the World?* (Baker, 2005), p. 63.
2. Taken from Kenneth Brockley, 'Egypt', *Echoes* mission magazine.
3. Although I have visited garbage village myself, I am also indebted to Rebecca Atallah of the Egyptian Bible Society for this information.

2. It's all about relationship

1. Taken from A. M. Hunter, *Interpreting the Parables* (SCM, 2012).

3. Dead men walking

1. Dietrich Bonhoeffer, *The Cost of Discipleship* (SCM, 2001), p. 7.
2. C. T. Studd (1860–1931) was a British cricketer and missionary, and one of the 'Cambridge Seven' (seven Cambridge students who became missionaries to China).

3. A. T. Pierson, *George Müller of Bristol: His Life of Prayer and Faith* (Waymark Books, 2011), p. 367.

4. John Stott, *Evangelical Truth* (IVP, 2003), p. 89.

5. Eric Metaxas, *Bonhoeffer: Pastor, Martyr, Prophet, Spy* (Thomas Nelson, 2011), p. 532.

6. Ibid., p. 531.

4. Who do you think you are?

1. Dallas Willard, *The Divine Conspiracy: Rediscovering Our Hidden Life in God* (HarperCollins, 1998), p. 207.

5. The Holy Spirit: Fruit and gifts

1. John Stott, *The Message of Galatians: Only One Way*, Bible Speaks Today (IVP, 1993), p. 148.

2. J. I. Packer, *Keep in Step with the Spirit: Finding Fullness in Our Walk with God*, 2nd edn (IVP, 2005), p. 70.

6. Mind the gap

1. P. A. Marshall, 'Work', in David J. Atkinson and David F. Field (eds.), *New Dictionary of Christian Ethics and Pastoral Theology* (IVP, 1995), p. 1020.

2. Timothy Dudley-Smith, *Authentic Christianity: From the Writings of John Stott* (IVP, 1995), p. 294.

3. Anthony A. Hoekema, *The Bible and the Future* (Eerdmans, 1979), p. 280.

4. Cited in James D. Bratt, *Abraham Kuyper: A Centennial Reader* (Eerdmans, 1998), p. 488.

7. Sex

1. See http://www.safetynet.org.uk/thefacts.php (accessed 23 February 2015).

2. Josh McDowell, *Beyond Belief to Convictions* (Authentic, 2005).

3. Joyce Huggett, *Dating, Sex and Friendship: An Open and Honest Guide to Healthy Relationships* (IVP, 1985), p. 28.

4. *Leadership* (Winter 1988), p. 12.

5. Cited in R. Kent Hughes, *Disciplines of a Godly Man* (Crossway, 2006), p. 22.

6. Cited in Gertie Mayeux, *Reflections of One Small Candle* (AuthorHouse, 2012), p. 81.

7. John Stott, *The Message of Thessalonians: Preparing for the Coming King*, Bible Speaks Today (IVP, 1994), p. 81.

8. Ibid., p. 81.

8. Money

1. Andrew Walker, *Telling the Story: Gospel, Mission and Culture* (Wipf & Stock, 2004), p. 143.

2. Michael Duduit, *Joy in Ministry: Messages from Second Corinthians* (Baker, 1989).

9. Time

1. Gordon MacDonald, *Ordering Your Private World* (Highland Books, 2013).

2. For more on this, visit www.virgin.com/richard-branson/the-way-you-work-is-going-to-change.

10. Work

1. Transcribed from 'The Table Podcast: A Biblical View of Stewardship', http://www.dts.edu/thetable/play/biblical-view-stewardship/ (accessed 27 April 2015).

2. Timothy Dudley-Smith, *Authentic Christianity: From the Writings of John Stott* (IVP, 1995), p. 244.

12. Community

1. Ronald Sider, *The Scandal of the Evangelical Conscience: Why Are Christians Living Just Like the Rest of the World?* (Baker, 2005), p. 96.

2. Jonathan Lamb, *Integrity: Leading with God Watching* (IVP, 2006), p. 78.

13. Mission

1. Rosemarie Jarski, *The Funniest Thing You Never Said: The Ultimate Collection of Humorous Quotations* (Ebury Press, 2004), p. 380.
2. This idea is reflected in the quotation: 'Preach the gospel at all times. Use words if necessary.' The saying, often mistakenly attributed to St Francis of Assisi, suggests that proclaiming the gospel by example is more virtuous than actually proclaiming with one's voice.
3. John Piper, *Let the Nations Be Glad: The Supremacy of God in Missions* (IVP, 2003), p. 17.
4. J. I. Packer, *Knowing God* (Hodder & Stoughton, 1975), p. 146.
5. Timothy Dudley-Smith, *Authentic Christianity: From the Writings of John Stott* (IVP, 1995), p. 315.

A final word

1. Dietrich Bonhoeffer, *The Cost of Discipleship* (SCM, 2001), p. 7.

KESWICK MINISTRIES

Our purpose

Keswick Ministries is committed to the spiritual renewal of God's people for his mission in the world.

God's purpose is to bring his blessing to all the nations of the world. That promise of blessing, which touches every aspect of human life, is ultimately fulfilled through the life, death, resurrection, ascension and future return of Christ. All of the people of God are called to participate in his missionary purposes, wherever he may place them. The central vision of Keswick Ministries is to see the people of God equipped, encouraged and refreshed to fulfil that calling, directed and guided by God's Word in the power of his Spirit, for the glory of his Son.

Our priorities: Keswick Ministries seeks to serve the local church through:

- **Hearing God's Word**: the Scriptures are the foundation for the church's life, growth and mission, and Keswick Ministries is committed to preach and teach God's Word in a way that is faithful to Scripture and relevant to Christians of all ages and backgrounds.
- **Becoming like God's Son**: from its earliest days the Keswick movement has encouraged Christians to live godly lives in the power of the Spirit, to grow in Christ-likeness and to live under his lordship in every area of life. This is God's will for his people in every culture and generation.
- **Serving God's mission**: the authentic response to God's Word is obedience to his mission, and the inevitable result of Christ-likeness is sacrificial service.

Keswick Ministries seeks to encourage committed discipleship in family life, work and society, and energetic engagement in the cause of world mission.

Our ministry

- **Keswick: the event**. Every summer the town of Keswick hosts a three-week Convention, which attracts some 15,000 Christians from the UK and around the world. The event provides Bible teaching for all ages, vibrant worship, a sense of unity across generations and denominations, and an inspirational call to serve Christ in the world. It caters for children of all ages and has a strong youth and young adult programme. And it all takes place in the beautiful Lake District – a perfect setting for rest, recreation and refreshment.
- **Keswick: the movement**. For 140 years the work of Keswick has impacted churches worldwide, and today the movement is underway throughout the UK, as well as in many parts of Europe, Asia, North America, Australia, Africa and the Caribbean. Keswick Ministries is committed to strengthen the network in the UK and beyond, through prayer, news, pioneering and cooperative activity.
- **Keswick resources**. Keswick Ministries is producing a growing range of books and booklets based on the core foundations of Christian life and mission. It makes Bible teaching available through free access to mp3 downloads, and the sale of DVDs and CDs. It broadcasts online through Clayton TV and annual BBC Radio 4 services. In addition to the summer Convention, Keswick Ministries is hoping to develop other teaching and training events in the coming years.

Our unity

The Keswick movement worldwide has adopted a key
Pauline statement to describe its gospel inclusivity:
'for you are all one in Christ Jesus' (Galatians 3:28). Keswick
Ministries works with evangelicals from a wide variety of
church backgrounds, on the understanding that they share
a commitment to the essential truths of the Christian faith
as set out in our statement of belief.

Our contact details

Mail: Keswick Ministries, Keswick Convention Centre,
Skiddaw Street, Keswick, CA12 4BY, England
T: 017687 80075
E: info@keswickministries.org
W: www: keswickministries.org

related titles from IVP

Mission Matters
Love says go
Tim Chester

ISBN: 978-1-78359-280-7
176 pages, paperback

The Father delights in his Son. This is the starting point of mission, its very core. The word 'mission' means 'sending'. But for many centuries this was only used to describe what God did, sending his Son and his Spirit into the world. World mission exists because the Father wants people to delight in his Son, and the Son wants people to delight in the Father.

Tim Chester introduces us to a cascade of love: love flowing from the Father to the Son through the Spirit. And that love overflows and, through us, keeps on flowing to our Christian community and beyond, to a needy world. Mission matters. This book is for ordinary individuals willing to step out and be part of the most amazing, exciting venture in the history of the world.

'If you want to fire up your church with a vision for global mission, this is your book! ... It should carry a spiritual health warning.'
David Coffey OBE

'I am sure this book will provoke many to respond to the challenge as they realize that there are still thousands waiting to be introduced to the Saviour.' Helen Roseveare

Available from your local Christian bookshop or **www.thinkivp.com**

related titles from IVP

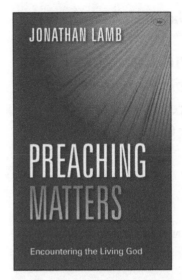

Preaching Matters
*Encountering
the Living God*
Jonathan Lamb

ISBN: 978-1-78359-149-7
192 pages, paperback

Preaching matters. It is a God-ordained means of encountering
Christ. This is happening all around the world. The author recalls
the student who, on hearing a sermon about new life in Christ,
found faith which changed his life and future forever; and the
couple facing the trauma of the wife's terminal illness who
discovered that Christ was all they needed, following a sermon
on Habakkuk.

When the Bible is faithfully and relevantly explained, it transforms
hearts, understandings and attitudes, and, most of all, draws us
into a living relationship with God through Christ.

This is a book to ignite our passion for preaching, whether we
preach every week or have no idea how to put a sermon together.
It will encourage every listener to participate in the dynamic event
of God's Word speaking to his people through his Holy Spirit. God's
Word is dynamite; little wonder that its effects are often dynamic.

*'A book for both preachers and listeners … a fitting manifesto not
just for the Keswick Convention, but for every local church.'*
Tim Chester

Available from your local Christian bookshop or **www.thinkivp.com**

related titles from IVP

The Amazing Cross

Transforming lives today

Jeremy & Elizabeth McQuoid

ISBN: 978-1-84474-587-6

192 pages, paperback

The cross of Christ is the heartbeat of Christianity. It is a place of pain and horror, wonder and beauty, all at the same time. It is the place where our sin collided gloriously with God's grace.

But do we really understand what the cross is all about? Or are we so caught up in the peripherals of the faith that we have forgotten the core? We need to ask ourselves:

- How deep an impact has the cross made on my personality?
- Do I live in the light of the freedom it has won for me?
- Am I dying to myself every day, so that I can live for Christ?
- Do I face suffering with faith and assurance?
- Can I face death in the light of the hope of the resurrection?

The authors present us with a contemporary challenge to place all of our lives, every thought, word and deed, under the shadow of the amazing cross, and allow that cross to transform us here and now.

'It is an ideal introduction to the heart of the Christian gospel, and a very welcome addition to the Keswick Foundation series.'
Jonathan Lamb

Available from your local Christian bookshop or **www.thinkivp.com**

related titles from IVP

KESWICK STUDY GUIDE 2015

The Whole of Life for Christ

Becoming everyday disciples

Antony Billington
& Mark Greene

ISBN: 978-1-78359-361-3
96 pages, booklet

Suppose for a moment that Jesus really is interested in every aspect of your life. Everything - the dishes and the dog and the day job and the drudgery of some of the stuff you just have to do, the TV programme you love, the staff in your local supermarket as well as the homeless in the local shelter, your boss as well as your vicar, helping a shopper find the ketchup as well as brewing the tea for the life group, the well-being of your town and the well-being of your neighbour ...

Suppose the truth that every Christian is a new creature in Christ, empowered by the Spirit to do his will, means that Christ is with you everywhere you go, in every task you do, with every person you meet ... Suppose God wants to involve you in what he's doing in the places you spend your time day by day ... Suppose your whole life is important to Christ ...

He does.

These seven studies will help you explore and live out the marvellous truth that the gospel is an invitation into whole-life discipleship, into a life following and imitating Jesus.

Available from your local Christian bookshop or **www.thinkivp.com**

Keswick Study Guides by IVP

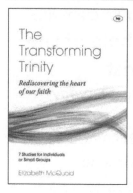

The Transforming Trinity
Rediscovering the heart of our faith
Elizabeth McQuoid

These seven studies will help you grow in your understanding of the inexhaustible riches of the Trinity. Find out why the Trinity is central to our beliefs and fundamental to the working out of our faith. Learn to worship the triune God more fully, reflect his image more clearly, and experience his transforming power in your life. Learn what it really means to know the Father, follow the Son, and walk in the Spirit. Because the Trinity is at the heart of Christian faith and life.

'A feast for individuals and Bible study groups.'
Sam Allberry

ISBN: 978-1-84474-906-5 | 80 pages, booklet

Really?
Searching for reality in a confusing world
Elizabeth McQuoid

These seven studies help us go deeper into the truth we are offered in Jesus Christ, and to root our lives in it. Because Jesus offers us himself, a reality that satisfies not only our intellectual curiosity, but also the deepest longings of our hearts. He offers us true security and sure hope for the future. He reshapes our thoughts, our life, our identity and our purpose. Real truth is found in Jesus Christ, and knowing him changes everything.

'Really? is a great resource to explore how the Christian message enables us to live with real confidence in the real world.' Tim Chester

ISBN: 978-1-78359-158-9 | 80 pages, booklet

Available from your local Christian bookshop or **www.thinkivp.com**

For more information about IVP
and our publications visit

www.ivpbooks.com

Get regular updates at **ivpbooks.com/signup**
Find us on **facebook.com/ivpbooks**
Follow us on **twitter.com/ivpbookcentre**

Inter-Varsity Press, a company limited by guarantee registered in England and Wales, number 05202650. Registered office IVP Bookcentre, Norton Street, Nottingham NG7 3HR, United Kingdom. Registered charity number 1105757.